Osborne
A Teacher's Handbook
Rosemary Cooper and Jennie Fordham

The marriage of Princess Alice to Prince Louis of Hesse, 1862.

Contents

Why visit Osborne?

Osborne House, terraces and fountain.

Osborne is almost entirely Victorian. It was designed, built and furnished for the royal family to their own specifications, and remains largely unaltered since Queen Victoria died here in 1901. It offers unique resources for those studying not only the Victorian royal family but other aspects of nineteenth-century life including architecture, art and design, technology, costume, education and leisure. The Indian Room, with its particular style, illustrates some Victorian attitudes towards the Empire and its peoples, and provides a way in to discussions with your pupils about the influences of other cultures.

Osborne is obviously not a typical Victorian home, but it can provide a useful comparison with other Victorian houses and styles of architecture which you might find in your own locality. It also provides an insight into the more personal aspects of Queen Victoria's reign, which are often difficult to convey in the classroom.

A visit to Osborne need not, however, focus entirely on history. The opening up of the estate, with the restoration of the royal children's gardens around Swiss Cottage, the Walled Garden and the terraces, allows your pupils to look at different aspects of the environment during their visit. There is scope for looking at the pressures placed on the house and grounds as a tourist attraction, as balanced against the need to protect the site and conserve it for the future. There are also opportunities for developing your pupils' writing skills as part of their visit, either through creative writing tasks or by setting activities which require factual or instructional writing. The *Educational Approaches* section of this book offers a range of ideas for activities across the curriculum for you to adapt and use with your pupils.

While your groups are inside the main house their activities will be based around using and developing their observation skills. Outside the house and in the grounds you will be able to develop investigative activities, with your pupils working in small, supervised groups.

Understanding the site

The story of Osborne

At the time of her marriage in 1840 Queen Victoria had three principal residences, Buckingham Palace, Windsor Castle and Brighton Pavilion. Since the royal family enjoyed being by the sea, a decision was made to abandon Brighton Pavilion in favour of a more private seaside residence. The Prime Minister, Sir Robert Peel, accordingly made some enquiries about properties on the Isle of Wight, a place which Queen Victoria had visited and greatly enjoyed in her childhood.

Buying Osborne

Old Osborne House, a handsome Georgian building owned by Lady Isabella Blachford, proved to be suitable (even to the royal physician who was sent to test the air), and in 1844 a year's lease was taken out on the house and grounds for a sum of £1,000. The house with sixteen bedrooms was small for a royal residence since large numbers of people were always in attendance on the royal family, but the Queen was delighted with it and decided to buy it.

After some bargaining, the house and grounds were bought for £26,000 together with Barton Manor, a neighbouring estate, and other properties for a further sum of £18,000. The Barton Manor estate generated income, and supplied produce to Osborne. The money was found from the Queen's own income rather than from state funds. In 1849 Brighton Pavilion was sold for £50,000, and much of this money was spent on furnishings for Osborne.

The alterations

Thomas Cubitt, the eminent builder who had elegantly developed large areas of London including Belgravia and Pimlico, was employed to undertake alterations and improvements.

The decision to employ a builder rather than an architect gave Prince Albert the opportunity he wanted to design and plan his own home. Initially the existing house was to be improved and enlarged but in fact it was eventually pulled down and a new house constructed. The Italianate style of the new Osborne with its two campaniles, or towers, was designed by Prince Albert who worked in close collaboration with Cubitt over the five years of its construction.

Building the Pavilion

Despite the building works the Queen and her family spent their first holiday at Old Osborne House in the autumn of 1844. In June 1845 the Queen placed a glass box containing coins of the realm under the foundation stone of a new block which was to be added to one corner of the old house. This was the Pavilion, which was to contain the Queen's

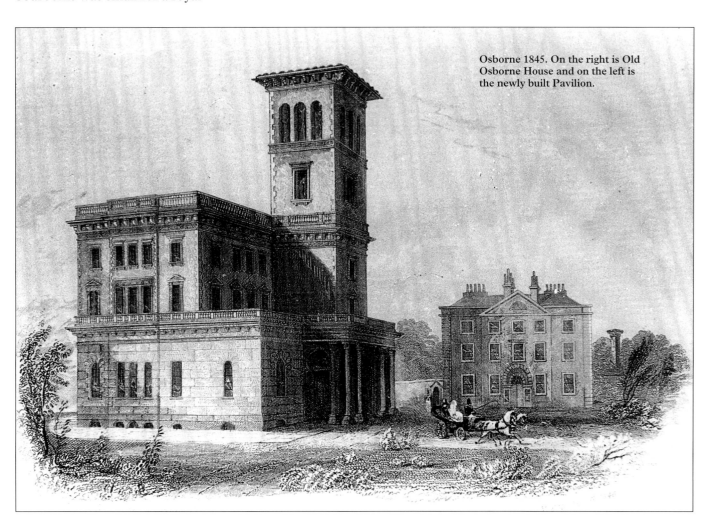

Osborne 1845. On the right is Old Osborne House and on the left is the newly built Pavilion.

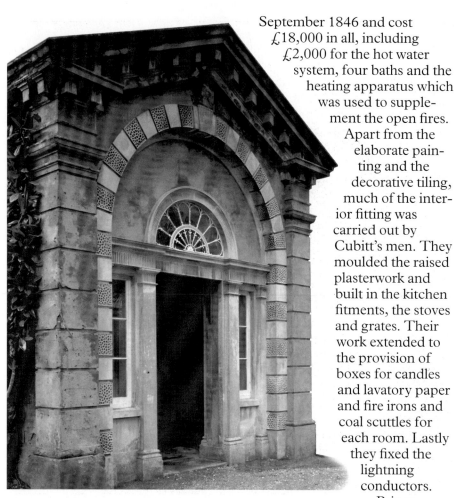

The only remaining part of Old Osborne House is the ornamental doorway, set into the wall of the Walled Garden.

September 1846 and cost £18,000 in all, including £2,000 for the hot water system, four baths and the heating apparatus which was used to supplement the open fires. Apart from the elaborate painting and the decorative tiling, much of the interior fitting was carried out by Cubitt's men. They moulded the raised plasterwork and built in the kitchen fitments, the stoves and grates. Their work extended to the provision of boxes for candles and lavatory paper and fire irons and coal scuttles for each room. Lastly they fixed the lightning conductors.

Prince Albert's artistic adviser, Ludwig Gruner, was put in charge of the interior decoration. He designed the elaborately coloured ceilings and walls in the classical manner of Greece and Rome. A London firm was employed to carry out the rich gilding and elaborate painting including the mock marbling in the stair hall.

Further building

The Pavilion was only the first stage of the plan. New wings were to be added in two stages. First the Household Wing was added for the accommodation of the ladies and gentlemen in waiting upon the royal family and, later, the Main Wing for guests and visiting members of the government. The Household Wing was sited behind the old house and a small corner of that building had to be demolished to make way for it. Late in 1847 the whole of Old Osborne House was pulled down and the Main Wing begun. The main doorway was removed and placed in the walled garden where it can be seen today.

In 1849 it was decided to build

a male servants' dormitory, known as the Barrack Block, behind the stables. This contained twenty-four wooden cubicles for liveried servants on the first floor and seventeen superior rooms for upper servants and a sick room on the ground floor. By 1851 the Household and Main Wings were completed and fully occupied. In the 1890s a maids' dormitory was built.

After Albert

The death of Prince Albert, from typhoid in 1861, at Windsor Castle, deeply affected Queen Victoria. She went into deep mourning and led a very secluded life for the next ten years. Very little happened at Osborne except for the regular visits of the Queen two or three times a year. Her routine changed after Albert's death, so that she could avoid being in the same place, at the same time of year, as she had been with Albert. She spent almost every Christmas at Osborne, to avoid Windsor. However, she stopped visiting Osborne on her birthday in May and on the Prince's birthday in August.

Victoria generally disliked change and over the years insisted that worn carpets and curtains be replaced with others of the same design. One small change was the provision of a smoking room for the gentlemen of the household in 1866. Smoking was generally disapproved of by the Queen and the room was placed at the end of the Household Wing with no entrance from the house so that gentlemen had to go outside to get into it. In 1880 a chapel was built on to the Main Wing to enable the Queen, a lifelong Christian, to attend church services within the house.

The Durbar Wing

The main innovation at Osborne after the death of Prince Albert was the building, in 1891, of a new wing on the west side of the house. This was to provide space for large receptions, which had previously been held in marquees on the lawn. Although conforming to the rest of the building on the outside, the inside was to be decorated in the exotic style of an Indian

private apartments.

The house was built of brick faced with cement or stucco and much thought was put into making it fireproof. The floors were laid on brick arches spanning iron girders and insulation was provided by a thick layer of cockle shells between the floors. Safety and efficiency were valued above showiness and many features of the house were surprisingly modest. The stairs and passages were made of expensive Portland stone but the skirting boards and mouldings were made of cement coloured to imitate stone. Oak floorboards were laid in the principal rooms only; elsewhere softwood was used. The principal windows were glazed with expensive newly-invented plate glass and the frames were made of mahogany, but elsewhere, cheaper glass and softwood were used.

The building of the Pavilion was completed in a remarkably short time considering that Cubitt had to start by opening a brickworks on the estate at Alverstone Cross. It was ready for occupation in

From 1903, Osborne was the home of the Royal Naval College. This picture, taken in 1909, shows Price Edward (later King Edward VIII) seated third left, and Prince Albert (Later King George VI) on the ground, centre.

Bhai Ram Singh, the designer of the Durbar Room. His work included carving the elaborate wooden moulds used for casting the plaster ceiling.

palace. The Queen had become Empress of India in 1876 and was enthusiastic about everything Indian. Bhai Ram Singh, an architect from the Punjab, was employed to design the interior, and the intricate plasterwork was carried out by a small group of British craftsmen over a period of two years.

Modern improvements

The Queen tried out both Bell's telephone and Marconi's wireless invention, and later telephones were used to connect various buildings on the estate. To make communication with ministers easier a telegraph office was set up in the basement. Electricity was laid on with the building of the Durbar Wing (the original electric lamp standards may be seen there), and eventually the whole house was wired. The power was supplied from a gas-driven generator in a battery house near the servants' barracks. As the Queen grew older and less able to walk, a lift was installed for her personal use. This was hand-operated by men stationed in the basement beneath the lift shaft.

After Queen Victoria

Queen Victoria's health was declining when she spent Christmas at Osborne in 1900. She suffered a slight stroke on 17 January 1901, and was nursed in her bedroom, surrounded by most of her family. On 22 January 1901 the Queen died. Her body lay in state in the Dining Room, until, on 1 February, the funeral cortege made its way to East Cowes, where the Royal Yacht Alberta was waiting to take the Queen back to the mainland. She was buried, alongside Albert, in the Royal Mausoleum at Frogmore.

In 1902 her son, King Edward VII, gave Osborne to the nation and the Royal Apartments were first opened to the public in 1904.

Part of the house was used as a convalescent home for officers of the Army and Navy. At the same time a Royal Naval College was established in the grounds. This trained naval cadets, including sons of the royal family, until its closure in 1921. English Heritage took responsibility for the site in 1986.

Site description

There are four distinct parts to the house, not all of which is open to the public. These are the Pavilion, the Main and Household Wings, and the Durbar Wing. There is a set route for visitors to the house, which can vary from time to time. This makes it a complex house to visit, as it is easy to become disoriented.

Before entering the house, take some time with your pupils in the central courtyard (originally a turning circle for carriages), looking at the different sections of the building (refer to the plan, right). If you stand facing the main portico, the Main and Household Wings are to your right, with the visitor entrance leading into the linking Grand Corridor. Originally the Grand Corridor had a completely open gallery, or loggia, above it, but this was later partly glazed to make the route less draughty for the Queen's ladies in waiting. The Pavilion is in front of you, with the Durbar Wing to the left.

Inside the house

You and your pupils will be asked to move from room to room fairly quickly, and there may not be time for your group to stand and look in detail at particular objects and paintings as they go round. In the following room descriptions, a selection of particular items has been described, to help you focus your pupils' attention on points of interest. Suggestions for observation work in the house may be found in the *Educational Approaches* section.

The Grand Corridor

Osborne House is entered through the doorway once reserved for distinguished visitors and members of the Royal Household. The Grand Corridor was intended to look impressive and was decorated in the classical style favoured by Prince Albert. The floor is laid with specially designed Minton tiles and the Latin word *SALVE* (greetings) was set into the floor by the entrance. The corridor was

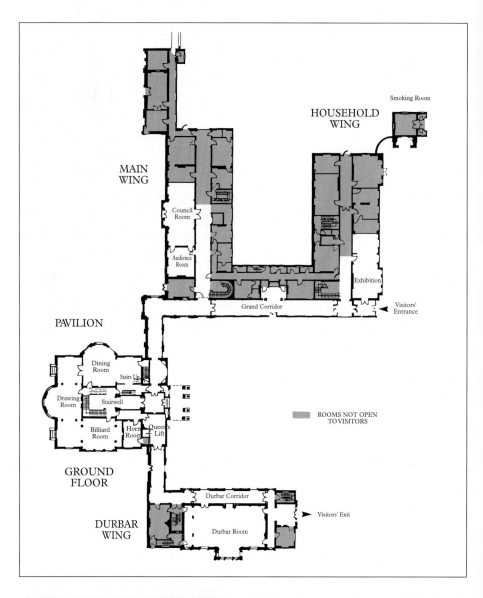

The Grand Corridor in 1867.
Notice the tiled floor.

designed as a sculpture gallery, and a niche contains a marble statue of Queen Victoria.

The Council Room

The Council Room was used for conducting state business when the Queen was at Osborne. At other times, the room was used for entertainment, including dancing, charades and drama by members of the Royal Household. The highly gilded and decorated interior was designed by Ludwig Gruner, Prince Albert's art adviser.
Look for:

■ the ornate chandelier with Minton porcelain candle holders supported by *putti* (cherub-like figures) and decorated with cupids

■ the portraits of Queen Victoria

The kitchen at Osborne, in 1876.

and Prince Albert, painted on Sevres porcelain, given by Louis Philippe, King of France, in 1846.

Queen's Audience Room

Distinguished official visitors were received by the Queen in this room.
Look for:

■ the writing desk, part of the original furnishings supplied in 1851

■ gilt satinwood chairs, upholstered in damask, also part of the original furnishings

■ the coloured glass chandelier decorated with convolvulus and arum lilies. Convolvulus was said to be the favourite flower of Prince Albert, whose childhood bedroom was decorated with convolvulus patterned wallpaper.

The Grand Corridor continues to the Portico, the Queen's entrance to the house. On the way notice the statue of Noble, one of the Queen's favourite collies.

The basement

An enormous amount of accommodation was needed for the maintenance of the household, and this was concentrated in the basement which housed the kitchens and sculleries, the beer and wine cellars, the silver pantry and all manner of store rooms.

The small back stairs lead down to the Table Deckers' area. You will first enter a small lobby, which had a hot cupboard to keep food from the kitchens, warm. The different courses were chalked up on to the cupboard doors so that the Table Deckers would know they had arrived. Then you will move into the servery area. This room was used to keep the china services for the Dining Room. These were made especially to be used at Osborne. The food was placed onto this china before it was taken up to the sideboards in the Dining Room.

The Table Deckers would prepare plans of where the guests would be seated. Once the Queen had approved the seating plan, it would be drawn out as reference for those waiting at table. They would then lay out the plates and glasses on the table. (The Yeoman of the Silver Pantry laid out the cutlery.) With larger tables, the Table Deckers would have to walk on the tops of the tables to set out the dishes. To avoid scratching the tables, they used to remove their shoes and wrap linen cloths around their feet.

Set squares would be used to find the centre line of the tables, along which the flower displays and some serving dishes were placed. The Table Deckers also used specially marked rods, to ensure that all the cutlery was put in exactly the right place, with the correct distance between place settings.

From the servery you are able to look into the room known as the Table Deckers' room. The cupboards contained all the glassware. The Table Deckers were responsible for washing, rinsing and drying all the royal family's china and glass. This was done using the two sinks in this room. Look for:

■ the decoration around the edge of the dinner service. Ask pupils if they can spot anything similar on walls and ceilings elsewhere in the house

■ different systems of lighting. Can pupils identify three ways of lighting the rooms?

■ the large silver centrepiece for the dining table

■ the large water filter, used to provide drinkable water for the family and household.

The small room to the left of the Table Deckers' room was used as a store. You then come back through the servery, and up the back stairs into the Dining Room. There is a sudden contrast of scale and decoration, and your pupils should notice the difference immediately.

The Dining Room

The Queen ate her meals in this room with guests or members of the Household. The food was served directly from the servery, via the narrow back staircase into the room. Princess Alice was married in this room in 1862 shortly after her father's death. Look for:

■ the large portrait by Winterhalter of the royal family as they looked when they first moved to Osborne. Five children are represented. In order of age they are: Victoria, Albert Edward, Alice, Alfred and

Helena. Notice that Prince Alfred is 'unbreeched', that is, wearing a dress

■ the portrait of Princess Beatrice, the Queen's youngest daughter shortly after Prince Albert's death. She is holding a miniature of her father

■ the large sideboard for holding dishes before they were served at the table. At Christmas it held a boar's head

■ the dining tables. One was brought from the Convalescent Home in 1901. The second, covered and dressed, table is a modern replica.

The Drawing Room
After dinner, Victoria would withdraw into this room, with guests or members of her household, for conversation, music or cards.
Look for:

■ the glass candelabra, shown at the Great Exhibition in 1851. They originally held candles but were later converted to electricity

■ marble statues of the royal children dressed as *'The Seasons'*, by Mary Thornycroft, one of the few women artists patronised by the Queen

■ the grand piano with twin stools. The Queen and Prince were both good musicians

■ a portrait of the Queen in early widowhood, by A. Graefle

■ the mirror shutters over the windows to act as double glazing and to reflect the candle light.

The Billiard Room
This room was used after dinner to play the fashionable game of billiards. It could be curtained off from the Drawing Room. Look for:

■ the entwined V and A symbol on the ceiling

■ the billiard table with decorative edging designed by Prince Albert

The nursery at Osborne in 1876.

the raised leather seat where the players could sit down (forbidden in the presence of the Queen unless specifically invited)

■ an inlaid marble table, designed as a chequer board, a gift from the father of Abdul Karim, the Queen's Indian Secretary

■ a rosewood cabinet, inset with miniatures of the Queen's nine children.

The Nursery Suite
The nursery rooms were conveniently sited on the second floor of the Pavilion, to give the Queen and Prince Albert easy access to their children from their first-floor apartments. The royal children used these rooms until they were around six years old, when they graduated to the schoolroom on the first floor. (The schoolroom is not open to the public.) The night nursery was used until the children were six, and then they moved to bedrooms in the main wing.

The Nursery Sitting Room
This room gives an introduction to the nursery area. It was originally the sitting room of Lady Lyttleton, Superintendent of the Royal Children. The adjoining room was her bedroom. In the 1880s the sitting room was made into a schoolroom for the children of Princess Beatrice, the Queen's youngest daughter.

■ the octagonal nursery table and chairs used by the royal children. Each chair has a high back with a shield containing the owner's initials

■ small chairs given to the royal children by the Queen's aunt, the Duchess of Gloucester, who embroidered the seat covers

■ marble limbs of some of the royal children made by Mary Thornycroft.

The Nursery Bedroom
This room has been restored as far as possible to its appearance in a photograph taken in the 1870s. The chintz fabric of the curtains was copied from scraps found under the covering of a child's chair at Osborne. Look for:

■ the cots. Two are replicas, but one is original; you can tell by the slightly different shape of the head and foot boards

■ a pedestal table bearing a wicker garden trug belonging to Princess Louise

■ a pair of dumb-bells (for exercise) engraved with the nameplate of Princess Helena

■ a child's high chair of bird's eye maple, part of the original nursery furniture

■ a reproduction doll's house based on one appearing in the 1873

photograph of the room

■ original building blocks used by the royal children

■ a crib hung with silk, used for Queen Victoria's children.

On the first floor are the private apartments of Queen Victoria and Prince Albert. These were closed off after the death of Queen Victoria, and were only opened to the public in 1954.

Prince Albert's Bathroom
This custom-built bathroom was a feature of the modernity of Osborne House. Water was raised to the house, initially by hand pumping and later with the aid of a steam engine. Waste was taken away through a brick arch sewer to a purification tank and then to the sea.
Look for:

■ the bath with mahogany lid. Water was let in and out through holes in the bottom. Notice the three taps for controlling the water

■ photographs of the royal children in tableaux representing 'The Seasons'

■ paintings on the wall by the young Prince Albert and Queen Victoria.

Prince Albert's Dressing and Writing Room
This dual function room was kept by the Queen very much as it was in the Prince's lifetime.
Look for:

■ the roll-top desk containing the Prince's writing materials, including black-edged stationery used after the death of the Queen's mother, sealing wax and paperweights

■ the umbrella stand with collection of walking sticks

■ Prince Albert's harmonium. The Prince used this instrument for composing when he was at Osborne.

The Queen's Sitting Room
Crowded with mementoes of the family and friends, this room was used by the Queen for her work and correspondence.
Look for:

■ twin desks used by the Queen and Prince Albert. The white bell-pulls worked by battery-powered electricity

■ a spinning wheel made in Scotland and a statuette of the Queen using it accompanied by her collie, Sharp

Prince Albert's bath.

■ a portrait of Queen Victoria nursing baby Arthur on the terrace at Osborne.

The Queen's Dressing Room
This room was used by the Queen for changing her clothes, to suit the occasions of the day, a procedure which required the help of dressers. After Prince Albert's death the Queen wore only black.
Look for:

■ the built-in bath which could be screened by mirrors when not in use

■ the shower, operated by hand from a previously hoisted container of water. Notice the large black thermometer for testing the water temperature

■ the monogrammed Minton dressing table set, a birthday present to the Queen from Prince Albert

■ the water closet under a mahogany lid

■ Queen Victoria's medicine cabinet.

The Queen's Bedroom
This room was entered from the Dressing Room through a concealed door in the wardrobe.
Queen Victoria died in a small couch bed in this room on 22nd January 1901, and remembrance services attended by members of the royal family were held here for some years after her death.
Look for:

■ the bed with tester (canopy) and hangings and the bronze memorial plaque commemorating the Queen's death. The bed is not short but only appears so because of its height

■ the replica of the silk pouch in which Prince Albert kept his fob watch; Queen Victoria kept the original on the bedhead after his death

■ the birthday table with tortoise feet made with ebony inlaid with mother of pearl.

The Page's Waiting Room
This alcove, on the first floor landing, was used by pages waiting to attend any summons from the Household. It now contains a portrait of the Queen's first grandson, Wilhelm II of Germany, on a visit to Osborne in 1889.

The Stair Hall
The Stair Hall is a good place to see the classical decoration chosen by Prince Albert for the formal areas of the house. A statue of the Prince in classical dress can be seen at the head of the stairs. The Stair Hall was decorated with plasterwork painted to resemble marble. There are two heating radiators, which conducted warm air from the boilers in the basement. This ingenious system circulated hot water through four-inch cast iron pipes slung between the basement ceiling and the ground floor. Hot air given off by the pipes rose through the flues in the walls via grilles to the principal rooms.

The Horn Room
This small room, on the ground floor, was used by the Queen as an informal sitting room. She some-

times breakfasted here when it was too cold to eat outdoors as she preferred. The room contains its original wallpaper and carpet, and is kept closed to protect these items. The horn furniture was bought by Prince Albert in 1846. The style became popular after similar furniture was displayed at the Great Exhibition in 1851.

Look for:

■ the German chairs made of deer antler

■ a table inlaid with sections of horn

■ the chandelier of deer antlers.

The Durbar Corridor
This corridor contains many objects and paintings relating to India, collected after the Queen became Empress of India in 1876.
Look for:

■ the lift which was added for the elderly Queen's use in 1893. It was hand-operated by men stationed in the basement

■ two large portraits by Winterhalter, the famous court German painter, of Princess Gorumma and Maharajah Duleep Singh, Indian exiles who were under the Queen's patronage

■ the portrait of Abdul Karim, the Queen's Indian Secretary.

The Durbar Room
The Durbar Room was built in 1891-93, to make space for large receptions which had previously been held in marquees on the lawn. The name Durbar is derived from an Indian word, meaning both a state reception and a hall for such receptions. The room originally contained Indian dining furniture, but this was disposed of in 1909. The room now contains many of the objects given to Victoria to mark her jubilees in 1887 and 1897. Many of the pieces show the same intricate style as the room itself.
Princess Beatrice, the Queen's youngest daughter, lived with her family in the rooms above the Durbar Room. These are not at

The Durbar Room, in the 1880s.

present open to the public.
Look for:

■ the portrait of Bhai Ram Singh, architect of this room

■ the plaster ceiling in Indian style

■ Indian decorative symbols, including Ganesha, the elephant god of good fortune, and the peacock, symbol of the Indian Mogul emperors

■ the balcony, with enough space for small orchestra if required for special entertaining

■ the brass lamp-standards, part of the original fittings. Electricity was installed when the Durbar Wing was built and these are examples of early electric lighting.

The Estate
Cubitt was responsible for a good deal of building throughout the estate including the lodges, the icehouse, greenhouses, sewers and wells. The planning and directing was done by Prince Albert, who had very clear ideas about what he wanted to achieve. A formal terraced garden was laid out below the Pavilion, with geometric flowerbeds between paths. These terraces have now been restored. Like other Victorian gardens, those at Osborne are decorated with statues. On Pavilion Terrace you can see a cast bronze life-size statue

of Prince Albert's favourite greyhound Eos. This was modelled by the Prince himself. There are also statues representing the four seasons.
The Walled Garden functioned in the eighteenth century as the kitchen garden for Osborne, providing fruit, vegetables and cut flowers for the house. In Victoria's time, vegetables and fruit came from Barton Manor and the Walled Garden produced flowers. This garden has been replanted to a contemporary design by Rupert Goldby, inspired by Victorian plants and planting. The Victorian glasshouses are also being restored.
Osborne, like most large Victorian houses had an ice-house. These were used to keep ice dug out of lakes during the winter months, and to keep rooms and food cool during the summer. The ice-house at Osborne was built on a north facing slope, in shady woodland. Like a wide, shallow well, about four metres across and nine metres deep, it has a cavity wall for insulation and holes in the floor to allow water to drain away. The top is covered by a brick dome and an earth mound, with an opening for filling it.
Thousands of trees were planted, including foreign and ornamental species.
For details of the children's area, including Swiss Cottage, see *Resource Sheet 5*.

Documentary sources

There is a wealth of documentary material available on Victorian life in general and the life of the royal family at Osborne in particular. You will find additional material in publications listed in the *Bibliography*.

Queen Victoria's view

The Queen kept a private diary in which she recorded both events and her personal feelings. The manuscript was edited and rewritten by Princess Beatrice after Victoria's death and the original in the Queen's own handwriting was destroyed. Letter writing was also a much more significant part of life then than it is today. The Queen kept in touch with family members and her government ministers through regular correspondence. Many of these letters survive.

'It is impossible to imagine a prettier spot – valleys and woods which would be beautiful anywhere; but all this near the sea (the woods grow into the sea) is quite perfection; we have a charming beach quite to ourselves. The sea was so blue and calm that the prince said it was like Naples.'

(Letter from the Queen to Lord Melbourne, 1845)

'Drove down to the beach with my maid and went into the bathing machine, where I undressed and bathed in the sea (for the first time in my life) where a very nice woman attended me. I thought it was delightful until I put my head under water, when I thought I would be stifled.'

(Queen Victoria's Journal, 1847)

'After dinner we went to the Council Room and saw the telephone. A Professor Bell explained the whole process which is most extraordinary. It had been put in communication with Osborne Cottage and we talked with Sir Thomas and Mary Biddulph, also heard some singing quite plainly. But it is rather faint and one must hold the tube rather close to one's ear.'

(Queen Victoria's Journal, 1847)

Members of the household

Members of the household also kept journals, wrote memoirs and corresponded with friends, revealing details of the lives of the royal family from another point of view. Sarah Spencer, Lady Lyttleton, was the Lady Super-intendent of the Royal Children, and thus a useful source on family life at Osborne. Frederick W Gibbs was the Prince of Wales' tutor. The Honorable Eleanor Stanley and Marie Adeane were Maids of Honour.

'Jan 27. In the morning it was difficult to fix his [the Prince of Wales'] attention on his arithmetic. The music with Mrs Anderson was not a good lesson. In the evening I read the story of Robert Bruce to him. I was astonished by the eager interest he took in it. Feb 28. Last Thursday the two sons of Mr Van de Weyer came to play with the Princes. They were eager and excited. (Next day) he became violent because I wanted some Latin done. He flung things about – made grimaces – called me names, and would not do anything for a long time.'

(Diary of F W Gibbs, 1852)

'Nobody caught cold or smelt paint, and it was a most amusing event coming here. Everything in the house is quite new, and the dining room looked very handsome. The windows lighted by the brilliant lamps in the room must have been seen far out to sea. After dinner we rose to drink the Queen's and Prince's health as a housewarming, and after it the Prince said, very naturally and simply but sincerely, 'We have a hymn' (he called it a psalm) 'in Germany for such occasions. It begins' – and then he quoted two lines in German which I could not quote right meaning a prayer to bless our going out and coming in. ...we all perceived that he was feeling it.'

(Letter from Lady Lyttleton, 1846)

'August 24th. Nothing to be recorded. – The weather still beautifully fine and warm; & only one shower today to interrupt its serenity – I regret to say that yesterday the Princess Royal told an untruth – asserting that I had desired she should walk out after supper in her pink bonnet – which I had not done, nor even mentioned the subject. – She was imprisoned with tied hands, and very seriously admonished; & I trust was aware of her fault in the right way. In other respects, these two or three days have been rather well spent – Her Royal Highness ate mutton again today at her own request – Her appetite & state of stomach generally are exactly in the usual rather imperfect and fluctuating state, with every symptom of high health besides. – The cold bath has been in constant use since the cold disappeared. – The Prince of Wales perfectly well always – and very good on the whole, excepting a childish fancy occasionally, such as wishing to get into his bath the moment he has left it, which being naturally refused, led to a roar yesterday evening; but only for a moment.'

'The children dine and tea in the garden to their hearts' content and yesterday evening they washed a basketful of potatoes and shelled a ditto of peas, which they are to cook for themselves today if they are good. Did you ever hear of such happy children?'

(Hon Eleanor Stanley, 1848)

Pictures

Paintings, engravings and photographs are all invaluable sources, and you will find examples throughout this book. The limitations of technology meant that photographs of people were usually posed, and are therefore less useful as a source on life and activities than they would be for today. However, information about life at Osborne can be extrapolated from photographs of the building and the estate; and artists' impressions, in paintings and published as engravings, sometimes shed light on human activity.

Rustic fête, given by the Queen to the workmen and labourers at Osborne House, to celebrate his Royal Highness Prince Albert's birthday.

Servants' hall.

Queen Victoria's sitting room.

12

"The Queen's favourite fruits were oranges, pears and monster indigestible apples, which would have daunted most people half her age, but she enjoyed them, sometimes sharing a mammoth specimen with Princess Beatrice, but more often than not coping with it alone… The Queen's dinner was timed to last exactly half an hour. I usually managed to satisfy my hunger but could not enjoy the excellent fare handed out so expeditiously.'

(Marie Adeane, 1887)

Printed material on Osborne

Osborne House was a place of national interest. Articles on it appeared in magazines and journals, and it was described in contemporary books. It also featured in local guidebooks and directories.

Using the documents

Many of the documents refer to places and things which can still be seen or for which evidence can still be found. Allocate documents or parts of them to pairs of children, and ask them to look out for evidence of any details that are mentioned and underline them. Alternatively, this could be done from memory after the visit. Examples might be: the bathing-machine, the dining-room with its windows towards the sea, the children's gardens, the geometric gardens and the statues. Read your pupils the description of Osborne from the directory of 1859. After the visit, ask pupils to write a brief description of Osborne for a modern guide-book.

Use the accounts written by the Queen's household, referring to the royal children. What do they tell us about the health, diet, education and discipline of the royal children? Which aspects of the royal children's lives at Osborne would your pupils find enjoyable or otherwise? Follow this discussion by asking your pupils to write a letter to one of Victoria's children describing what is different about their own upbringing.

Use the documents and the picture of the servants' hall, to find out about the lives of those who were employed by the Queen. How can you tell that some servants were much more important than others? Where did Lady Lyttleton dine? Where did the third and assistant Table Deckers dine? Compare the photograph of the servants' hall with the Dining Room.

Make a selection of sources suitable for your pupils and display or reproduce them. Ask them to think about their usefulness to historians, by choosing the best source for particular purposes: for example, a book on Victorian childhood, a biography of Prince Albert or Queen Victoria.

'The Palace stands about a mile from the shore, and is a magnificent structure, in the Palladian style of architecture… The terrace gardens are laid out geometrically, and are adorned with a great variety of statues, vases, busts, fountains and seats… The gardens and pleasure-grounds are on a scale of princely magnificence, and are designed with great ability, and stored with the rarest of ornamental shrubs. The interior of the palace displays the same exquisite taste which reigns without. It is furnished and decorated in the most elegant manner… The Billiard Room, which is also the Reception Room, contains a splendid billiard table, of enamelled slate, by Magnus, and is furnished in a superb manner, in amber satin and gold. Its ceiling is handsomely painted, and the walls adorned with a number of valuable pictures, amongst which are Cardinal Wolsey entering the gate of Leicester Abbey… About half a mile from the Palace, in a secluded part of the park, is a beautiful Swiss cottage, built entirely of wood, in true Alpine fashion… Here the younger members of the Royal family spend much of their time, and are permitted to throw off some of the restraint of royalty… They each have a set of garden tools and a plot of ground…

Directory of Hampshire and the Isle of Wight,
William White, 1859

'The Duty of the Table-decker is to superintend the arrangement of Her Majesty's table: placing everything in perfect order before the dinner is served. The Assistant Table-decker lays the table cloth for the Queen's Luncheon, and arranges the tables. At the Queen's breakfast, this duty is performed by the Footmen. They have also to wash all the decanters, glasses etc used at the Queen's table; they are in charge of the pickles, bread etc; order up the napkins and tablecloths for breakfasts, lunches and dinners, from the Housekeeper etc. There are three Table-deckers, with an assistant, and a Wax-fitter. Sleeping rooms are provided for them in the house. The first and second Table deckers dine in the Steward's room; the third, the Assistant, and the Wax-fitter, take their meals in the Servants' hall. Their travelling expenses are defrayed, when their services are required, upon the removal of the Court. Their salaries will average as follows: First Table-decker, £200; Second, £150; Third, £90; Assistant, £52; Wax-fitter, £52.'

Sketches of Her Majesty's Household, published by
William Strange, 1848

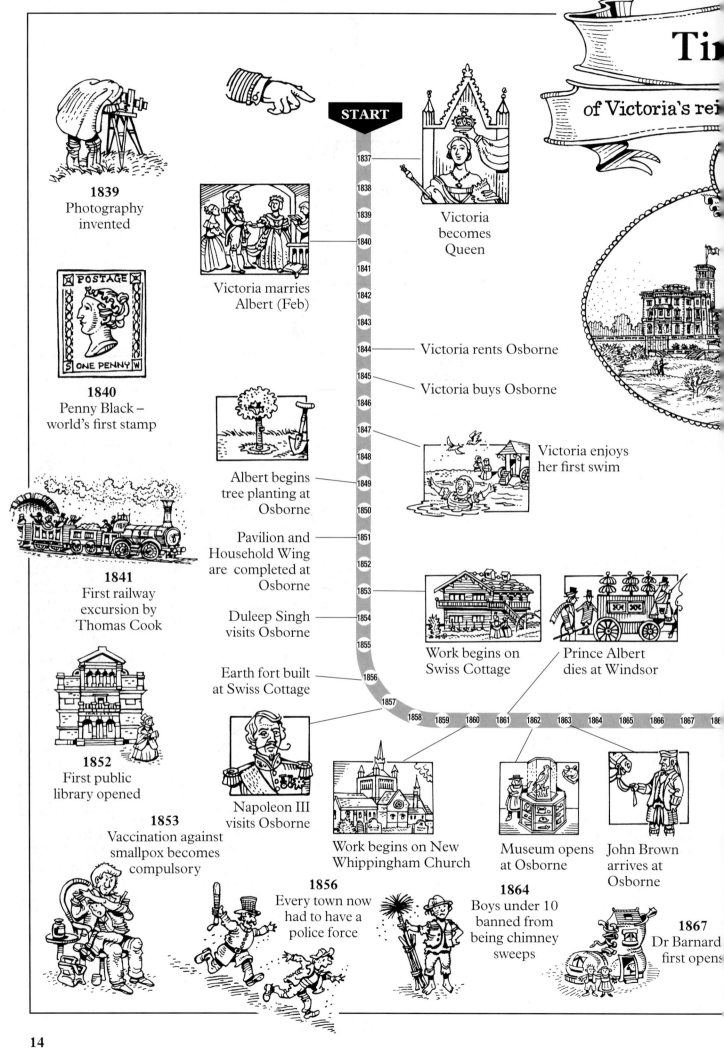

1839
Photography
invented

POSTAGE
ONE PENNY

1840
Penny Black –
world's first stamp

1841
First railway
excursion by
Thomas Cook

1852
First public
library opened

1853
Vaccination against
smallpox becomes
compulsory

Victoria marries
Albert (Feb)

Albert begins
tree planting at
Osborne

Pavilion and
Household Wing
are completed at
Osborne

Duleep Singh
visits Osborne

Earth fort built
at Swiss Cottage

Napoleon III
visits Osborne

1856
Every town now
had to have a
police force

Victoria
becomes
Queen

Victoria rents Osborne

Victoria buys Osborne

Victoria enjoys
her first swim

Work begins on
Swiss Cottage

Prince Albert
dies at Windsor

Work begins on New
Whippingham Church

1864
Boys under 10
banned from
being chimney
sweeps

Museum opens
at Osborne

John Brown
arrives at
Osborne

1867
Dr Barnard
first opens

1837 1838 1839 1840 1841 1842 1843 1844 1845 1846 1847 1848 1849 1850 1851 1852 1853 1854 1855 1856 1857 1858 1859 1860 1861 1862 1863 1864 1865 1866 1867 186

OSBORNE HOUSE
ISLE OF WIGHT

Osborne House, built for Queen Victoria as a country retreat is a unique resource for the study of Victorian royal family and of many other aspects of nineteenth century life. The buildings and the objects they contain challenge powers of observation, deduction and expression and may stimulate a variety of activities extending across the curriculum.

Historical Description

Osborne House was designed by Prince Albert in collaboration with Thomas Cubitt, the eminent builder. The main part of the house is placed around an open courtyard. The centre block or Pavilion completed in 1846 has the dining room, drawing room and billiard room on the ground floor. On the first floor are the private apartments of Queen Victoria and Prince Albert. The block which contains the Durbar room was the only major addition to the royal palace after Prince Albert's death. Its interior is decorated in exotic Indian style.

Also to be seen at Osborne is Swiss Cottage, the playhouse of the royal children, the Museum and the individual productive gardens each child tended. Swiss Cottage was built to house objects collected by and given to the royal children and grandchildren. A miniature fort built largely by the young Prince Arthur is also nearby as is Queen Victoria's bathing machine, which allowed her, in 1847, to take her first dip in the sea.

The historic landscape and gardens around the house, were designed by Prince Albert They are currently under restoration with the formal terraces displaying Victorian parterres bedded out with period plants. Visitors are able to explore much of the landscape and see the developments in progress.

Learning Opportunities

Beautifully preserved, Osborne allows us a rare glimpse into royal family life in the nineteenth century. As well as a study of Queen Victoria and her family life at Osborne, other aspects of Victorian life such as architecture, art and design, technology, work, costume, education and leisure can be explored here.

A visit would make a very substantial contribution to a **History** study of the Victorians, at all Key Stages. For example, portraits seen here will help pupils discover information about dress; objects and architecture will give a sense of Victorian taste and skill. There would also be opportunities to develop work in **Technology** after studying some of Prince Albert's latest design features.

Because much of Osborne is unchanged from the time that Victoria and her family lived there, it is an ideal site for pupils to study details of the life of a Royal family. **Preparation** should include familiarisation with the members of the family, through family trees and photographic sources. Many of the sources in the Document Pack (see Resources) could be studied both before and after a visit in order to put the house in a context, and to help 'people' the site.

There is so much to see **on site**, that it may be advisable to set groups of pupils specific enquiries based on one aspect, such as the nursery and the children; leisure activities or Queen Victoria's mementos of travels round her Empire. Older pupils may respond well to a form of problem solving or challenge, which could be designed to fit a range of subjects in the curriculum; an open ended but focused task.

Detailed suggestions for a further range of activities are provided in the teachers' handbook including ideas for follow up work such as making optical toys and Victorian games.

The house may also develop children's imagination through role play and drama in **English**, and the opportunity to **follow up** back at school by creating their own 'Victorian' documents; letters, diaries and photographs. Issues of conservation might also be raised and the large number of visitors may lead to a study in **Geography** on the impact and issues of tourism. For children on a residential visit to the Isle of Wight, Osborne could be part of a study of the Island as a whole, or of themes connected to the sea and the coast. The garden lends itself to many National Curriculum topics relating to the sciences. The garden at Swiss

Cottage is a designated Heritage Seed Library Garden growing historic varieties of vegetables and fruit organically. There are many landscape features which could be explored by educational groups, such as the parterre, walled garden, vine alley, shrubbery and avenue.

Location
1m SE of East Cowes.
Note: Swiss Cottage, the fort and the museum are situated ¾m (20 mins walk) from the house. A carriage ride operates but school parties generally prefer to walk.

How to get there
Bus: For timetable information about buses fromRyde, East Cowes and Newport which stop at the Gates of Osborne House ring Southern Vectis Coaches 01983-827005.
Boat: For details of ferry services to Isle of Wight destinations, contact the Isle of Wight Tourist Office, tel 01983-524343.

Opening hours
1 April-31 October: daily 10am-5pm

Facilities
Access for the disabled: To the exterior and ground floor of the house. Vehicles with disabled passengers may set them down at the entrance to the house
Education Centre: A working base for schools studying Osborne House: this has slides, documents and relevant objects including Victorian toys and costume for educational use. Notes on the room's contents are available when you make your booking. The education centre must be booked in advance.

Parking: Free car park near house.
Refreshments: School parties are asked to use the picnic area close to Swiss Cottage
Shop: Guides and booklets, postcards, souvenirs.
Toilets: On site including one for disabled persons.
Note: There is a set route which visitors must follow. In the high season, May/June for schools, it is crowded. It is not possible to double back on the route or to stop and draw.

Free Educational visits
Educational visits to English Heritage Historic Properties are free if prebooked at least fourteen days in advance via Osborne House, see below. **Limit on party number:** 100 max, from any one educational establishment in one day.
Staff-pupil ratio: at least 1 to 15

Contacts
Booking and site information: Education bookings,

English Heritage, Osborne House, East Cowes, Isle of Wight, PO32 6JY, Tel: 01983 280201.
Regional Education Officer : Jennie Fordham, English Heritage, Historic Properties South East, 1 High Street, Tonbridge, Kent TN9 1SG. Tel: 01732-778000.
Isle of Wight College: St Mary's Passage. Warwick Street, Ryde, PO33 2EG, Tel: 01983 812927

Nearby and Related sites
Whippingham Church is a small nineteenth century church nearby which was used by Queen Victoria and her family whilst at Osborne.

A guide to resources
Tolhurst M. Teachers' Handbook: Osborne House, A practical handbook for Teachers, English Heritage, 1986 (revised 1990), ISBN 1-85074-289-8
Tolhurst M. Document pack: Life on a Royal Estate, English Heritage, 1986, ISBN 1-85074-126-3
Fry P.S. Osborne House, Souvenir Guide English Heritage, 1985, ISBN 1-85074-111-5
Osborne House, Guidebook English Heritage, 1989 (revised 1991), ISBN 1-85074-249-9
Victorian Osborne 12 slides and notes English Heritage 1987
Durbin, G. A teachers Guide to Using Historic Houses . English Heritage 1993 ISBN 1850 74 3908
All English Heritage resources are available by post from English Heritage, PO Box 229, Northampton, NN6 9RY Tel:01604 781163 (24 hours) Fax: 01604 781714
Girouard M. Life in the English Country House, Penguin 1980 ISBN 01 400 5406 5
Note: For an extended bibliography, see teacher's handbook.

English Heritage Education Service
Our Education service aims to help teachers at all levels make better use of the resource of the historic environment. Education groups can make free visits to over 400 historic properties managed by English Heritage. The following booklets are free on request.
VisitingHistoric Sites contains details of all English Heritage properties and a booking form, and is packed with ideas and activities for National Curriculum study and work on site. Our **Resources** catalogue lists all our educational books, videos, posters, and slide packs. Please contact:

English Heritage
Education Service
Freepost 22 (WD214)
London SW1E 5YY
Tel: 020-7973 3442
Fax: 020-7973 3443
www.english-heritage.org.uk.
September 2000

Activity Sheet 1

Classical collection

Osborne is built in a style that was often used for grand houses in Britain at the time. The style was copied from buildings people saw in Italy. The details came from classical architecture, which used ideas from Greek and Roman buildings.

How many of these details can you find on the outside of Osborne? Use a different colour for each detail and shade them on the drawing of the house. Shade the boxes with the relevant colour to make a key.

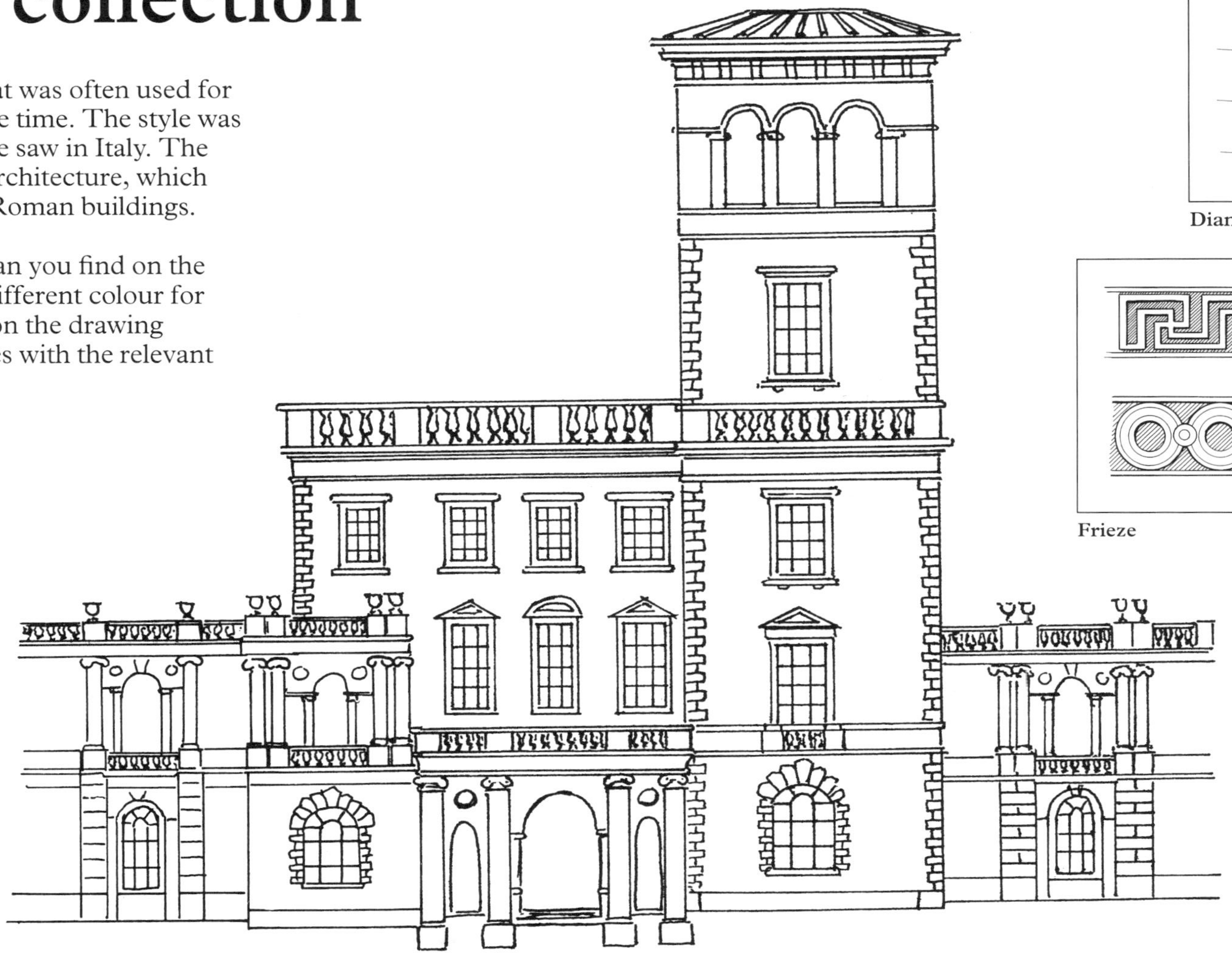

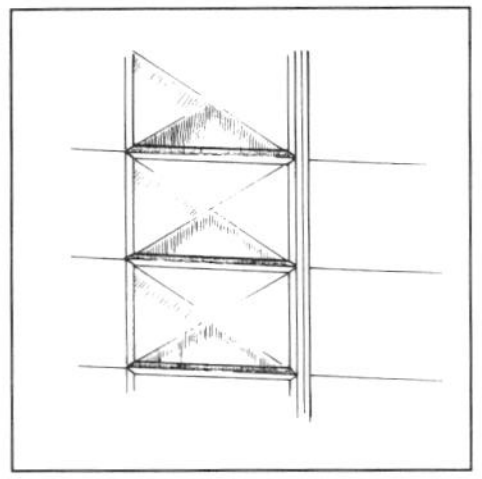

Diamond-faced blocks

Frieze

Pediment

Balustrade

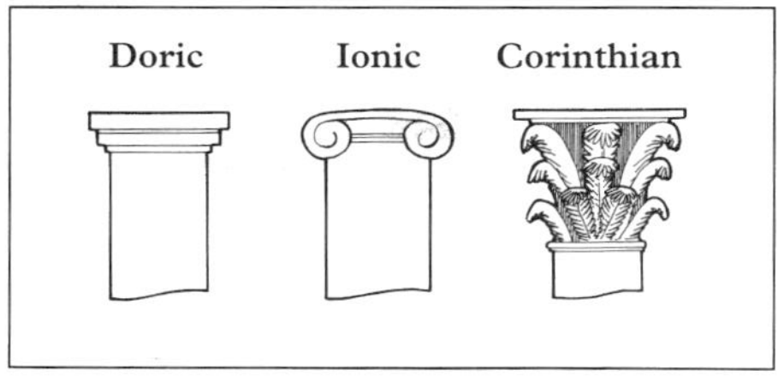

Doric   Ionic   Corinthian

Decorated capitals

Urn

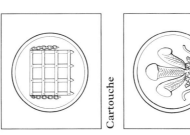

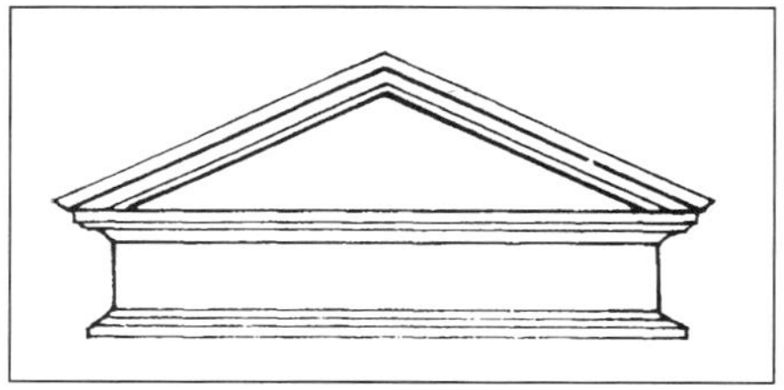

Cartouche

Cartouche

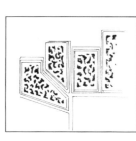

Rustication

Opinions of Osborne

Fill in what you think these people might say about Osborne. The unlabelled one at the end is for your own view.

Prince Albert

Lady in waiting

Household servant

An important visitor

Gardener

Out of the ordinary

Look out for these objects as you tour the house. As you find each of them, draw a line to one of the labels to show what it is made of.

The most surprising object I saw was

_____

The most interesting object I saw was

_____

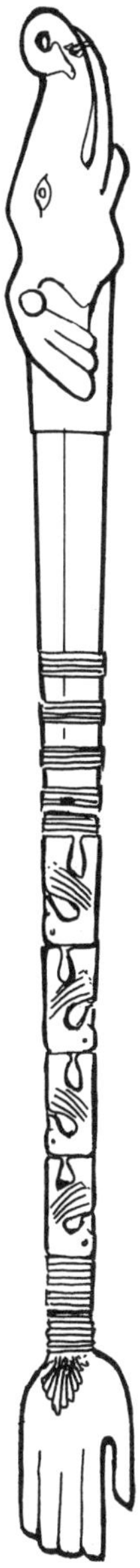

antler

wood

silver

stone

ivory

glass

china

© English Heritage Education

Tree study

Choose a tree to study carefully. Use this sheet to record as much information as possible about your tree.

Ring the word which describes your tree, or record the information on the chart below.

Position on site	sheltered open/exposed	sloping ground flat ground	wet ground dry ground
Surrounding environment	dense woodland parkland	thin woodland mown grass	scrub/bushes/brambles bare ground
Measurements	height	girth (1.5m from ground)	
Approximate age			
Shape	short spreading horizontal branches	tall narrow upright branches	drooping branches
Management	natural clipped	pollarded pleached	coppiced

Leaf shape (sketch)	**Flower** (sketch)	**Fruit** (sketch)

Bark	rough furrowed	smooth colour	peeling
Commemorative plaque	Take a rubbing		
Identification			
Origin	British native	foreign (from which area?)	

ine

Osborne House

END

1901
1900
1899
1898
1897
1896
1895
1894
1893
1892
1891
1890
1889
1888
1887
1886
1885
1884
1883
1882
1881
1880

Victoria dies at Osborne

The Boer War begins

Bhai Ram Singh finishes decoration of Durbar Room

The Kaiser visits Osborne

Victoria becomes Empress of India

70   1871   1872   1873   1874   1875   1876   1877   1878   1879

1896
Marconi first demonstrates his wireless (radio)

Victoria's Diamond Jubilee

Work begins on the Durbar Room Electricity is introduced to Osborne

Victoria's Golden Jubilee and Abdul Karim (the Munshi) comes to Osborne

1889
A 14mph speed limit on motor cars

1881
Many houses and streets lit by electricity

1867
Telephone invented by Alexander Graham Bell

1870
Education made compulsory for children up to 10

1874
Factory Act sets 10 hour maximum working day

Queen Victoria's family tree

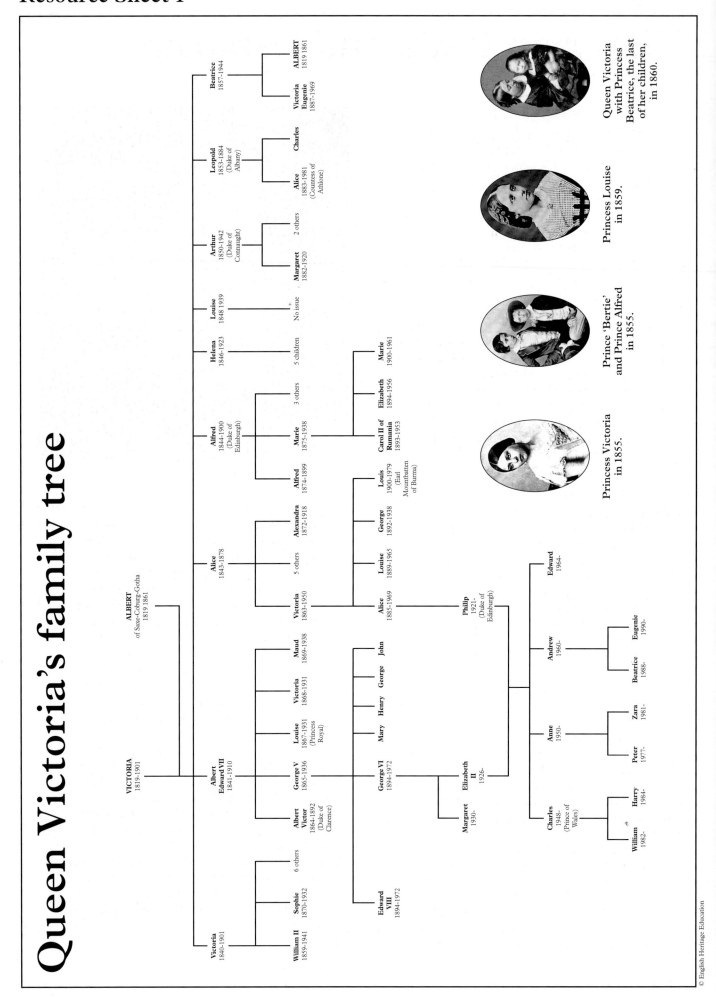

Queen Victoria with Princess Beatrice, the last of her children, in 1860.

Princess Louise in 1859.

Prince 'Bertie' and Prince Alfred in 1855.

Princess Victoria in 1855.

© English Heritage Education

Victorian India and Osborne

Queen Victoria had had contact with Indian Maharajahs since quite early in her reign, one of whom was Duleep Singh, the last Maharajah of Lahore. He was entertained by Victoria and Albert at Osborne when he visited England in 1854, aged fifteen.

When the British took control of the Punjab in 1849, Duleep, then only ten years old, had given up his claim to the throne in return for a large pension. At this time the Koh-i-noor diamond, one of the largest in the world, was taken from him by the East Indian Company. The diamond was then given to Queen Victoria, and became part of the Crown Jewels. Later, Duleep Singh was given the diamond to examine by the Queen, after it had been cut and faceted. This was a tense moment, as her courtiers were not sure how he would react, but he returned the diamond personally to the Queen as an act of courtesy. This took place while he was being painted for his portrait by Winterhalter, the Queen's favourite portrait painter; this painting now hangs in the Durbar corridor at Osborne.

Princes Arthur and Alfred in Sikh dress, in 1854.

The Queen and her Indian Servants

When Queen Victoria was proclaimed Empress of India in 1876 her interest in the area increased. In a letter to Lord Lansdowne, who was then Viceroy of India, she wrote *'The Queen-Empress is much interested by his description of his tour, and is very jealous of all that he has seen, for she would give anything to visit India.'*

As a gift on the occasion of her Golden Jubilee, in 1887, Victoria was given a pair of Indian servants. The Queen herself designed their uniforms, as was traditional in the Household. For Balmoral the costume was in tweed, cut Indian style, and when serving dinner they wore white with gold turbans and trimmings. She also had Indian chefs. It was their job to prepare a curry for every luncheon.

The Queen's passion for all things India also spread to the design of her home. In the 1890s she had the Durbar Wing built onto Osborne House. The room was designed in the Indian style, by Bhai Ram Singh. He had been specially brought to England on the recommendation of Lockwood Kipling, the father of Rudyard Kipling. The ceilings and walls were covered in ornate plaster decorations, imitating the marble carving found in the palaces of the Mogul emperors and Hindu temples. The carpet was made in Agra, specially for the room, and the chairs and light fittings were all designed to match.

Abdul Karim

Of all her Indian servants, Hafiz Abdul Karim was Queen Victoria's favourite, and there are several portraits of him hung in the Durbar Corridor at Osborne. He came to England from Agra in 1887 for the Queen's Golden Jubilee. First he worked as a waiter, but was controversially promoted into the gentlemanly class of her household when he was made her Indian Secretary. She even allowed him to blot her letters (always a sign of special favour) and took lessons in Hindustani from him. Because of this he became known as the *munshi* (Hindustani for teacher).

His promotion displeased the rest of the Court, because he had crossed the unbridgeable barrier between the lower servants and the royal household. Eventually he sat next to the ladies in waiting at royal events, and had a carriage to himself during outings. This led to anger and intrigue, and the members of the household tried to have him demoted. The Queen, though, remained loyal. Karim was important to her exactly because he was far removed from the British establishment, and the Queen felt she was getting much closer to understanding the heart of India.

© English Heritage Education

Indian food

Queen Victoria employed several Indian chefs. Their job was to prepare the curry that was served each day for lunch. By the end of the nineteenth century curries, even in colonial India, would only have been served for breakfast or luncheon, never dinner.

The early British traders in India had quickly adapted to curry. When they returned home to England, they wanted to continue eating this familiar dish. It was not so easy to obtain all the right spices in England, so the idea of curry paste or powder developed. The quality of these varied, but Queen Victoria's Indian chefs would not have dreamed of using them.

One of the European chefs of the royal household wrote: '...*Nor would they use the curry powder in stock in the kitchens, though it was of the best imported kind, so part of the Household had to be given to them for their special use and there they worked Indian style, grinding their own curry powder between two large stones and preparing all their own flavouring and spices.*'

On the right is a recipe for curry spices and their use, as they would have been prepared in the 1880s. The Hindi words for the ingredients are also given.

Curries were not just made in India in the nineteenth century, they were also found in other countries like Malaya and Ceylon (now Sri Lanka). These curries were slightly different to their north India counterparts, as they were made with larger quantities of coconut milk, and were therefore milder and more delicately spiced. Similar to these were the curries or Moli made by the Tamils of southern India, who mainly made vegetarian curries. Even today it is our lack of understanding which means that we do not realise that many of the 'Indians' who make curries on our high streets come from places like Bangladesh, and that curries come from places as far apart as the Caribbean and Afghanistan.

The British also brought their own culinary inventions to India. Soup was a British dish, unknown in India. The most famous Anglo-Indian soup is Mulligatunny (now spelt Mulligatawny), made up from the Tamil words *molegoo* (pepper) and *tunnee* (water). In India the basic ingredients of a thin, spicy liquid would have been made up and eaten with rice as a meal in itself. But the British got their Indian chefs to add meat and thicken the liquid with butter and flour, and created a soup instead.

The English and the Moguls were not the only foreign invaders to influence Indian cuisine. The Vindaloo is actually derived from a dish of pork marinaded in wine vinegar called vinha d'alhos, brought by the Portugese when they first arrived in Goa in 1496. The locals just added more garlic and spices to flavour it. However, the Vindaloo curries made in Indian restaurants in Britain have a very different composition. The earliest Indian restaurants in Britain were run by Punjabis, who found that there was a demand for hot curries. Most Punjabis prefer highly flavoured but mild curries, but they had no problem making their own standard curries hotter by adding one or more teaspoonfuls of chilli powder. They needed smarter names for their dishes and looked for inspiration to southern India. Vindaloo was used, although the British restaurant version bears no relation to its Goan namesake.

1880s Curry powder recipe

4lbs.	of turmeric	*huldi.*
8lbs.	of coriander-seed	*dhunnia.*
2lbs.	of cummin-seed	*jeera.*
1lb.	of poppy-seed	*khush-khush.*
2lbs.	of fenugreek	*maythi.*
1lb.	of dry-ginger	*sont.*
½lb.	of mustard-seed	*rai.*
1lb.	of dried chillies	*sooka mirreh.*
1lb.	of black pepper corns	*kala mirreh.*

Using the amounts above, when finally mixed, the powder will fill about half-a-dozen pickling bottles.

To use this powder, first fry garlic and onions in butter, to which you add the curry powder, along with wine, coconut milk and stock. This makes the curry stock or gravy. Then lightly fry the meat, take it off the heat and marinade for half an hour in the curry gravy. Then put it to the heat again in a stewpan with the gravy and simmer, boiling it down or reducing it to the required moistness, checking the stock for flavour at this stage, in case a little more spices or bay leaves are required.

Children's Osborne

Swiss Cottage

The royal children laid the foundation stone for Swiss Cottage in 1853. The house was pre-fabricated, and then assembled in position, just as many houses are today. It was handed over a year later, on Queen Victoria's birthday. The house was designed to be much more than a play house. It was to be part of the children's education. Cookery, housekeeping, gardening and woodwork were all taught here.

On the ground floor the cottage has a pantry and a kitchen, where the royal children could practise cooking.
Look for:

■ the wood-fired range with warming cupboards, meat spits and brass tap for the water supply

■ the charcoal-fired range for hot-plate cookery

■ a dresser containing copper utensils specially made for the royal children

■ the slate-lined sink.

The first floor is reached by an outside staircase and the balcony. It contains a dining room, dressing room, sitting room, lobby and its own WC.
Look for:

■ the writing desk, with its stationery, silver seal stamped 'Swiss Cottage', quills and blotting book

■ the model shop 'Spratt, Grocer to Her Majesty', with counter, scales and heavily laden shelves

■ pressed seaweed and shells collected by the royal children

■ a cradle in the shape of a boat, bought by the Queen in 1895 at a church bazaar

■ a carved writing desk bought by Prince Albert at the Great Exhibition in 1851. It opens by turning a handle and has secret drawers.

The Museum

All children like to collect things, and Victoria's children did too. Sometimes they were given presents by visitors to Osborne, but many items they found for themselves. They kept their collection in Swiss Cottage until it grew too large. The museum was then built in 1862. It was re-arranged in 1916, and the objects are displayed

Swiss Cottage, in 1920.

today in the same way
Look for:

■ two Egyptian bronze cats for holding mummified kittens.

■ a five-legged deer, originally from Windsor Great Park, looked after at Osborne by Princess Beatrice.

Gardens at Swiss Cottage

Prince Albert remembered his own childhood garden, and wanted his own children to have the same experience. Plots were laid out around Swiss Cottage for each royal child. They were expected to tend the fruit, flowers and vegetables themselves, although the younger children would have had some help.

If the children produced a good crop of vegetables, the under-gardener presented them with a certificate and Prince Albert would buy the vegetables from them at market prices.
Look for:

■ the children's tools, all initialled, in the thatched garden shed.

The area was for play as well as work. A miniature fort and barracks were built, and an animal house and paddock were provided for the children's pets.

The Fort

The miniature earth fort was finished in 1856. The Albert Barracks, built of small bricks especially made on site, was added in 1860. It was largely constructed by Prince Arthur whose ambition was to be a soldier.

© English Heritage Education

The Queen's servants

The Queen had maids and footmen like many other noble families, but also had Ladies and Lords waiting on her as Ladies in Waiting and Equerries. Below these were the professional servants, such as her Doctor and the Treasurer of the Household, and beneath these were the more usual servants, such as the housekeepers, cooks, coachmen, pages, grooms and attendants on the royal children.

Local people were also employed to carry out any extra work. Many of these were employed year after year. The Queen would often employ others from the same family if one person had proved reliable.

The following imaginary letters, based on people who were at Osbone, and recorded in the 1881 census give you an idea of what their lives were like.

Osborne
15 March 1861

Dear Charlie,
You said you would like a little description of the work that I do, as you wonder what it is that a Table Decker does. Well as you would guess, we are in charge of the decoration of and laying the Queen's table. This is not like ordinary tables, as it is the Queen's. Everything has to be just so.

We have a quiet morning, as the footmen are in charge of the Queen's breakfast, which in good weather she takes outside, H.M. is a right one for fresh air. My assistant, William Gower then starts to prepare the Queen's table for luncheon. But I am not idle. After breakfast the list of who is dining that evening comes down from Queen Victoria. It is from this that I work out where everyone should be seated. It is complicated doing this, and the Queen has her say of course, but it is mainly planned according to the "order of precedence". These plans I send to the footmen and diners.

I then decide how I should decorate the table, and order the flowers and fruit from the gardeners. But my work proper starts in the afternoon, when all my preparations take place. With large banquetzs, the work seems endless, and we even end up walking on the large tables, after the cabinet maker has made sure they are strong enough. I work out where to put the candelabra and my assistant hands them to me. At the great banquets in London we use the gold services, and some of the candelabra are the size of a man, so you can imagine how heavy they are. But at Balmoral and Osborne only silver is used, and everything is much smaller and cosier, like a holiday really.

I hope this answers your question. It seems along time ago since I saw you and Jane at our home, but I must say life is still as pleasant as it ever was.

I remain forever your loyal friend,

John

John Kirby – Table Decker, 38 years old, married, and from Ashley in Northamptonshire.

Osborne
April 22 1883

Mary,
The letters here come thick and fast as usual, and I am spending my time deciphering telegrams and the Queen's numerous memos in my room.

The Queen was tetchy today, and I had my work cut out calming H.R.H. the Duke of Connaught, when he received one such memo. It was written quite tersely, complaining that he ain't taking his duties in India as well as she might like, and that she feared his forthcoming stay there would be annoying the Viceroy. Alas, this was nothing compared to the anger of the Prime Minster, when he came down to Osborne this morning. I am sure he is aware that H.M. called him in immediately to see her, knowing full well that he was flustered from the journey.

These two events will provide quite an atmosphere at the Queen's Dinner tonight, but I am sure we can keep all amicable if the more difficult subjects are avoided.

I trust all is well at Windsor. Our youngest, Arthur, is continuing to acquit himself well here, he has quite taken to being the Queen's Page. God bless you.

Henry Ponsonby – Private secretary, 64 years old, and married with five children. He was born in Corfu, where his father was Governor.

Osborne
14 July 1856

My dearest brother Wilhelm,
On Friday 5th of January we travelled to Osborne, in the glorious Isle of Wight. The packing on the 4th shall be passed over in silence, because there is nothing agreeable and much that is disagreeable about it. A wardrobe maid and one dresser have to travel with the baggage, the other with the Queen. As you can see, we are quite the closest servants to the Queen. I was sent this time with the baggage, along with the wardrobe maid, Mary (a girl from Brussels). We and the luggage arrived two hours after the Queen.

At Osborne my room is called the tower room, and is on the third floor above the Queen, because of this my window has a most beautiful outlook over the sea. Here my thin size is an advantage, for space is in general limited, and we have very small rooms. However, the beds are not very big either, and thus a bigger one had to be arranged for me, so that I can lie full length.

My busiest time here is when the Queen is entertaining. We have our work cut out to keep up with events, collecting and ordering the gowns, shawls and jewellery so that the Queen is ready to receive her guests. An hour or so later we then have to get a whole new ensemble together for the Queen to wear at dinner.

I am writing this letter while the Queen is dining, as this is when I have time to myself. But my evening is often not over until after midnight, when we help the Queen retire, only to have to get up early in the morning ready to prepare the Queen and her clothes for the day.
I remain, as always,
your Loving Frieda.

Frieda Arnold – Dresser to Queen Victoria, from Carlsruhe in Germany, 26 years old, unmarried.

Marie Mallet – Maid of Honour, married with two children.

Osborne
July 20th 1897

My dear Bernard,
I cannot believe that it is time for my next month with the Queen to commence. It seems like no time at all since I was last on duty, and I miss you and dearest Victor and baby dreadfully.
I and my current 'pair' Mary Hughes, got down to Windsor very comfortably. At eight I dined with the Queen (a ladies' party) which I always think very pleasant as the Queen talks much more freely and gives her opinion in a most decided and amusing manner.
We then thought we were free for the evening, and retired to a quiet corner of the Queen's Drawing room, when suddenly Princess Louise came up to me and said 'You are to play'. So Mary and I seated ourselves at the piano and had to rattle off various duets which we had never seen before. I had a long talk with H.M. afterwards. She was as kind as ever and asked much about my illness and for news of Victor and the baby, adding 'I hear he is beautiful'.
I believe this house will be very full before long, all the Royalties like the country life and sea bathing. But for me life at Osborne is much less attractive, as there is less excitement and few grand banquets. I also miss the library at Windsor, but worst of all there is little accommodation for the Court and none at all for you and my dearest children.
Yours with deepest affection,

Marie

Educational Approaches

The educational approaches suggested in this section make use of different aspects of the house and estate, and link them to various curriculum areas. Each approach has an on-site activity, which forms its focus, together with preparation and follow-up work.

Classical collection

The architectural design of Osborne reflects what was fashionable at the time for a large country house. It was built in the 'Italianate' style, the traditional style of Italian villas. Though not strictly classical, the style owed a great deal to the legacies of Greece and Rome, including symmetry, proportion and classical details. In this approach, pupils will be looking at the overall design of the facades and the principles behind them, as well as the decorative details of the exterior. It provides an opportunity to look at the house in its setting and to consider some of the mathematical principles of design and decoration.

Preparation

Encourage your pupils to think about some of the principles of design by looking at the facades of your school and other buildings nearby – preferably ones that vary in size and status. Provide outlines and ask pupils to record the positions of doors, windows and decorative features. Discuss what they have observed and recorded. Is the arrangement regular or haphazard? Is it symmetrical? Are the windows all the same size? How much decoration is there? Are there any reasons for the arrangement? What is the function of the building? Do the features reflect the function in any way? For example, is the building meant to look important or imposing (like a town hall), or homely and welcoming (like a public house, perhaps)? Does the facade look as though it was planned, or has it evolved? Are there signs that it has been changed? If so, does this reflect a change of use?

If appropriate, reproduce classical details from *Activity Sheet 1* and set your pupils an observation exercise on buildings near your school. Ask them to find buildings which have any of these features. Most high streets have examples in their municipal buildings, banks, shops and offices. It may be possible to show that use of these features tend to reflect an important function. If your pupils have studied the Greeks, remind them of the origin of the classical style and discuss why it might have been favoured for imposing buildings.

Explain the classical principle of proportion in design – a principle that gives a visually satisfying result. In pieces of card, cut rectangular apertures measuring 8cm by 5cm. This aperture has the proportions of the 'golden rectangle'. Use these apertures to test the proportions of doorways, windows, and even whole structures: hold the card away from you and look through the aperture, moving the card back and forth until the aperture coincides with what you are testing. Take the cards with you to Osborne.

On site

Give pupils copies of *Activity Sheet 1*. Ask them to study the sketches of classical details and then find examples of them on the facade of Osborne House; they can then draw them in the correct places on the picture of the front of the house.

Extend your work on the exterior by asking pupils to record the mathematics that have been used in the building. List the different shapes that you can see. Study the proportions of the building and of its features, by using the prepared cards; use coloured pens to outline on the activity sheet the features that accord with the golden rectangle. Record the main lines of symmetry. Sketch examples of repeating patterns.

Go to the terrace at the back of the house. Here the building will look less imposing, but you should still find examples of the golden rectangle and observe the principle of symmetry. Here, too, you can see some of the same design principles extended into the surroundings of the house. Satisfying shapes are arranged in a pattern that continues the symmetry of the building, and decorative features of the architecture are echoed in the balustrades of the terraces. Give your pupils enlarged copies of the shapes used in the parterre on the terrace. Ask them to find out how many times each shape is used.

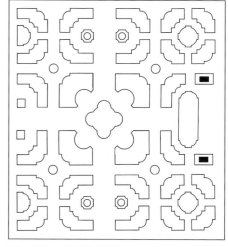

The parterre design.

Follow-up

Ask your pupils to design a facade for the front of an Italianate building. Specify the number of floors. Pupils should use the golden rectangle as much as possible and include the kind of classical features they have observed at Osborne.

Give pupils the shapes used in the parterre design. Ask them to cut out the correct number of each shape (as recorded during their visit) and arrange them on a sheet of paper in the pattern of the parterre. Pupils could follow this by designing their own symmetrical parterre using different shapes.

Opinions of Osborne

Your impression of a building will depend on your point of view. For example, a village farm labourer's cottage looked picturesque and cosy to the romantic artist, but actually living in it would have been a damp, draughty and squalid experience. What people felt about

Osborne House would have varied too. Queen Victoria herself thought it was *'really too lovely... the quiet and retirement all make it a perfect paradise – which I always deeply grieve to leave'*, but not everyone else would have shared that view.

In this approach, pupils try to see the house through the eyes of different people. It could be used to emphasise the contrast between life below and above stairs, or to illustrate something of the way in which the royal household functioned. It could also be used to summarise more detailed work on Queen Victoria at Osborne. It is more appropriate as a conclusion to a Victorian study than an introduction.

The activity sheet takes six key people, whose views could be added to the Queen's: Prince Albert, one of the children, a lady-in-waiting, a servant, a gardener, and an important visitor.

Preparation

The class will need to know that Osborne was the royal family's holiday home, but that even on holiday the Queen was still expected to undertake her royal duties: hence rooms for state functions, entertaining, and meetings (involving government ministers, ambassadors and foreign royalty and heads of state). They will also need to understand a little of how the royal household worked, with its courtiers in attendance on the queen, the hierarchy of servants, and the permanent staff and estate workers (see *Resource Sheet 5*).

Briefly discuss each of the people chosen for the activity. You could think about whether they were used to seeing such imposing buildings, what parts of the building they would have been able to view, what they actually did at Osborne, and whether their job would have made a difference to how they felt about it.

On site

Give out *Activity Sheet 2* before you tour the house to remind the children of the characters they are thinking about. Explain that they will not be expected to fill in the speech bubbles during their tour, but they will need to look and

remember in order to complete the sheet later. A piece of paper could be supplied for noting ideas. After the tour, discuss what they have seen and help them to apply it to the people on their sheet, perhaps feeding in information and questions like this: Prince Albert helped to design the house. Would he have been pleased with it? Is there any room in the house he would have particularly liked? What was the job of the Table Decker? Which rooms in the house did he know best? Fill in the speech bubbles on the activity sheets. One of the spaces on the sheet is left blank. The pupils can add their own comment in the speech bubble.

One of the rare photographs showing Victoria and Albert with all their children. It was taken at Osborne in 1857.

Follow-up

Ask pupils to develop their speech-bubble views by providing evidence for them. They could do this through more extended writing – a diary entry or letter, for example, or by recording a conversation or discussion between the characters, or by role-playing interviews with them.

Make a display of the different views people might have had. Put a picture of Osborne in the centre and representations of different characters around it. Give each character to a small group of pupils and ask them to write a suitable speech bubble. Follow this with a similar display of comments on the

house today, expressing the thoughts of the pupils (and adults) who visited Osborne in your group.

This approach is highly adaptable. You could take just one character, or two, to suit your teaching objectives, and adjust the activity sheet by enlarging pictures and speech bubbles. You could distribute the characters round the class, so that all are covered but each child focuses on only one: when you meet together for feedback, you could compare the different impressions the characters would have had. There are lots of alternatives to the people on the activity sheet: for example, a child on the estate, who might have seen the inside of the Indian Room at a Christmas party; an Indian prince; the local telegraph boy, who brought messages for the Queen; a servant with cleaning or fire-lighting duties. The scope could also be extended to include Swiss Cottage or the estate.

Palace and home

This approach looks at Osborne's role as both a family home and a royal palace. Thus it also looks at the way in which the house reflects the Queen's dual roles of monarch and mother, roles in which she was greatly revered in her lifetime. The pupils will be looking for evidence of Victoria's status as monarch, and also of Victoria and Albert's efforts to treat Osborne as a personal family home.

Preparation

Discuss with your pupils how they 'personalise' their rooms and how families give their own 'family' character to their homes. You could think about personal souvenirs and mementoes, things reflecting tastes and interests, family photographs, things that have been made by family members or friends.

Do some work on symbols and their use, for example symbols used in road signs and trademarks, religion and hobbies – symbols which take the place of a lot of words. Look at royal symbols and national symbols, for example the crown and heraldic lions.

Some preparatory work on the royal family and their use of Osborne would also be helpful. Look at how they catered for family life, with the Swiss chalet and the children's gardens, family picnics and home-made family entertainment.

Your pupils will also need to know that the work of government continually involved the Queen, and had to go on even when she had retreated to Osborne. The Prime Minister and other ministers had regular audiences with her; ambassadors and heads of state were frequent visitors. These people had to be reminded of her royal status even in the relative intimacy of her holiday home. Explain that some rooms at Osborne are therefore very impressive, while the royal family's private rooms are less grand.

On-site

Remind the class that Victoria and Albert wanted Osborne to be not just a palace, but a private family home, where their children would be able to enjoy a simpler and less formal upbringing than was possible at other royal residences. Ask them to look out for things that show us it was a family home –personal possessions, family mementoes, things that remind us of family life. Suggest that they choose two things to report back on – one from inside the house and the other from the grounds (including the Swiss Cottage area).

The royal children at Osborne, painted by Victoria in 1850.

Follow-up

Talk about the things they noticed. These could include family portraits, sculptures of the children, watercolours painted by the Queen, paintings and sculptures of the family's dogs, the children's gardening tools, the children's gardens. What evidence did your pupils see that Victoria and Albert encouraged their children to enjoy family life, to be active, and to work and play together?

Look together at the diary and journal extracts (see *Documents* section). Which of these documents also show that Osborne was intended to be a family home, which the children would enjoy?

Ask your pupils to use the evidence they saw during their visit, together with the evidence in the documents, to write a diary entry for one of the royal children, at the end of a day spent at Swiss Cottage and the garden.

Out of the ordinary

Osborne House contains an amazing collection of Victorian objects, illustrating the opulence and taste of the period. In this approach, pupils will be using observation skills to find seven different objects, each made from a different material. This activity could be done in connection with

work on materials, or it could be used to illustrate Victorian inventiveness, taste and decoration.

Preparation

Do some work on materials and their origins. Classify materials into animal, vegetable and mineral. Assemble collections of objects made from different materials, such as different kinds of metal. What materials did people use in the past, which are rarely used now, often for conservation reasons? (Examples might be ivory and crocodile skin.)

Bury some objects under the ground, for example a sheet of newspaper, a copper coin, a piece of cotton fabric, an old plate, a plastic beaker and an iron nail. Leave them as long as you can – several weeks if possible. Dig them up and note which have deteriorated. Look for other objects which show the ravages of time, such as worm-eaten wood, faded material, dog-eared books. Ask pupils to look out for objects in the classroom which show signs of wear and tear.

Which materials were available in Victorian times? Which of them deteriorate over time? Some materials need special care to prevent them from rotting, fading or corroding. What steps do your pupils think ought to be taken to protect the Victorian objects in Osborne House?

Investigate different methods of decorating materials and consider their suitability. For example, look at applying colour in the form of glaze or paint, shaping and moulding materials, incising patterns, carving. Are any materials decorative in their own right? Is their appearance enhanced by polishing?

Do some activities to practise observation skills.
Kim's game: place a selection of objects on a tray; allow pupils to look at them for a minute or so; cover them and ask pupils to list them.

Allow pupils to look at and talk about an object for a few minutes; remove it and ask the pupils to draw it from memory.

On site

Introduce *Activity Sheet 3* before you begin your tour. To complete the sheet you will need to visit the Swiss Cottage as well as the house, as one of the objects is in the museum there. As it simply requires pupils to find the object, identify the material and draw a line from the object to the label, it will usually be possible to complete the sheet on site.

Remind the pupils to look out for, and remember, other objects that are unusual and interesting. They can record their choices for particularly surprising and interesting objects at the end of the tour. Encourage pupils to respond individually to this part of the sheet, emphasising the validity of personal opinions.

Follow-up

Brainstorm a list of words and phrases to describe each of the objects on the sheet. Follow this by composing short poems, each line describing one of the objects. The results should say something about Victorian decorative objects and therefore about Victorian taste.

Make Victorian-style objects, using unusual materials and decoration. You could decorate small boxes with quilling or découpage or by sticking sea-shells on the outer surfaces. Mirrors or photograph-frames could be

Victorian crafts

Making a shell-framed picture.
You will need:

■ an old plate

■ a Victorian-style picture (greetings cards offer plenty of scope)

■ glue

■ household filler

■ sea-shells (washed and dried)

■ varnish

■ a piece of scrap card

■ some 'blu-tack'

■ water, an old container and a spoon for mixing filler.

Cut the picture into a circle of a suitable size to fit the centre of the plate. Cut the card into a circle of the same size and fix it with 'blu-tack' to the plate in the position you intend the picture to be. Mix a quantity of filler and spread it round the rim of the plate. (The card circle should protect the centre where your picture will go.) Press the shells in the filler in a suitable pattern, to make a frame for the picture. Arrange them as closely as possible. Remove the card circle. Leave the filler to dry. Varnish the shell frame and glue the picture in position.

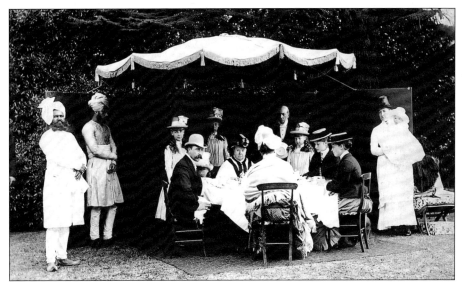

Queen Victoria, with her family and servants, in the gardens at Osborne.

decorated with shells. Small decorative cross-stitch designs could be worked and made into needle books or book covers. You could take inspiration from the fake-marble decoration at Osborne (on walls and pillars) and marble paper to decorate boxes and other appropriate objects.

The Victorians were great collectors. Osborne House reflects this acquisitive tendency. Victoria and Albert themselves collected works of art. The children amassed

an amazing eclectic collection of objects which had to have a building specially erected to house it. Many museums that flourish now owe their existence to the enthusiasm of a Victorian collector.

Children nowadays are often collectors. Discuss your pupils' collections. Some could be displayed in the classroom. This would be an opportunity to encourage the collector to classify the collection in some way and to provide appropriate labels.

The task: The Durbar Room is finished. Queen Victoria is delighted with the pure white, richly decorated walls and ceiling. She intends to use the room for the banquets she gives for important visitors. She has announced that she needs a new dinner service specifically for the Durbar Room. She would like the designs on the plates to have some connection with the decoration of the walls and ceiling. She has asked the members of your class to submit designs, from which she will choose one as the design for her new Durbar dinner service.

the Durbar Room is one room in the house where your pupils should be able to linger to observe and sketch. However, even in this location, you may not be able to gather them together to talk to them as a group, so you will need to spend time explaining the task before the visit.

Show pupils a picture of the room, and ask them to imagine it in use for a banquet. Discuss the Queen's likely requirements. The dinner service must clearly be designed for the room; the Queen will also want it to reflect her status as monarch and head of the world's biggest empire, so she will expect something grand and impressive.

colour schemes. The designs can then be reproduced on disposable cardboard plates, or even painted on second-hand plain china plates acquired from junk shops. If individuals opt for an unusual shape, the plate can be cut from plain white card.

Pupils should submit their designs to Queen Victoria, accompanied by some explanation, written or spoken: for example, what the design is based on, how it was developed, and why it would be suitable for the Queen. The task could become a competition, with someone to impersonate Queen Victoria and make a choice from a display of all the designs.

The Indian connection
The Indian material at Osborne is fascinating evidence for Victoria's interest in her empire. It is a useful resource for introducing this significant aspect of Victorian times and for looking at the influence of the art and culture of another part of the world.

Preparation
Look at a map of the world showing areas which were part of the British Empire. You could talk about why European countries had imperial ambitions: for economic reasons – as sources of raw materials and markets for manufactures; for reasons of status and influence – colonies provided bases for British troops all over the world; for idealistic reasons – some imperialists believed Britain had a duty to spread its civilisation and culture.

Provide some background information on India in the nineteenth century: the multiplicity of small states with their own princes as rulers, the religion of India, and the caste system. Explain the role of Britain as the imperial authority – the occupying army and the administration. Do some work on India and Indian traditions. You could look at Indian dress, make a collection of Indian objects, cook Indian food, *(see Resource Sheet 3)*. The on-site task makes use of the Durbar Room, added to the house to accommodate functions. The task takes advantage of the fact that

Replica menu, place cards and seating plan for a dinner at Osborne in 1898. The wooden table seating marker is a replica of one used by the Queen to arrange seating plans.

On site
Remind pupils of the task and give out sketching materials before they begin their tour.

Encourage them to make several sketches of motifs from the decoration.

The follow-up work suggested for this educational approach also makes reference to the Table Deckers' rooms, included in the tour of the house, and to the kitchen garden, which has been restored and may also be visited.

Follow-up
Develop the sketches into designs for plates. Think about colours and what would be appropriate, perhaps trying out a variety of

A royal banquet
There are many examples of Victorian recipes easily available. (See *Bibliography*.) Devise menus for a banquet in the Durbar Room. Design and produce menu cards using motifs from sketches done during your visit. They could be designed to match the plates or could reflect the decoration of the Durbar Room in another way.

Remind pupils of the Table Deckers' rooms, which they will have seen during their tour of Osborne. One of the Table Deckers' duties was to lay the tables for royal meals. All the place-settings had to be exactly the same distance apart. Ask pupils to lay a table with the plates all equally apart, and to find the exact centre of the table for a vase of flowers.

Remind pupils of the table centre-piece, an arrangement of fruit and flowers on a silver stand, which they will have seen in the Table Deckers' rooms. Fruit and cut flowers were supplied from the estate. Choose a time of year and ask pupils to find out what might have been available from the sheltered walled garden.

Trees

Trees – native and foreign – are a significant feature of the Osborne estate. They were planted as individual specimens and as clumps to improve the landscape, and were also managed as commercial woodland. This approach requires pupils to make a detailed study of an individual tree, using systematic observation and recording skills. The information collected can provide raw material for work in science, mathematics and environmental studies.

Preparation

Make a collection of fallen tree leaves to demonstrate the variety that exists. Do some bark rubbings to show how pattern and texture vary. Examine the colour of bark; is it always brown? If you can acquire suitable paint charts, you could try matching the colours to the paint samples. Do some sketches and silhouettes of trees in order to focus on their shape. Use reference books to identify a tree from its leaves, bark and shape.

Make sure your pupils understand the vocabulary used on the sheet, in particular the terms used in tree management. Devise a way of estimating height, for example by standing a pupil nearby and comparing the pupil's height with the height of the tree. Explain how trees grow in height and girth and how the girth measurement can give a rough guide to age.

Assemble the materials you will need: measuring tapes, sketching pencils, paper and wax crayons for bark rubbings, sketch-maps of the area you have chosen for the study – preferably a well defined area, such as the lawns to the west of the house.

On site

Divide the class into small groups

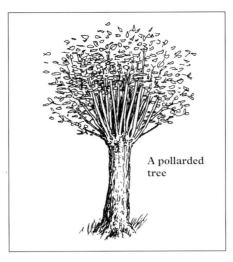

A pollarded tree

A coppiced tree

Pleaching was usually done to make an alley.

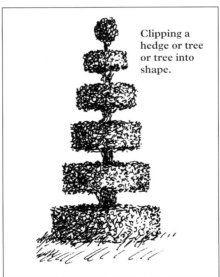

Clipping a hedge or tree or tree into shape.

and allocate a tree to each group. Ask them to mark the location of their tree on the sketch-plan, and to use the activity sheet to record their observations and findings. Identifying the tree does not matter initially, though it would be satisfying to include this information eventually.

Follow-up

Use reference books to find out more about your trees. If you can find their places of origin these could be marked on a map of the world. What sort of conditions would they enjoy in their native habitat – warm or cold, wet or dry, mountain or lowland? How different would conditions be at Osborne? Do you think this has made any difference to the way the tree has grown?

Classify and order the trees in various ways. They could be ordered according to height, girth or estimated age. They could be classified by leaf-shape, whether evergreen or deciduous, by type of fruit, or by bark texture.

Four seasons

This activity uses the grounds at Osborne as inspiration for creative writing. The activity sheet focuses on the formal parterre garden on the seaward side of the house, but you could do a similar exercise at other locations in the grounds. Pupils are encouraged to use their observations and imagination to produce short written pieces using sculptures of the four seasons as their starting-point. During the visit they will be collecting their own words inspired by the site.

Before the visit

The activity sheet assumes that pupils are familiar with the terms 'noun' and 'adjective'. You may like to give pupils some background information on the sculptures they will see. The four figures were given to Queen Victoria by Prince Albert at Christmas 1855 and on her thirty-seventh birthday the following May. They were made of zinc but were originally electroplated in bronze.

Discuss with your pupils how the changing seasons may be depicted. Pictures on calendars, for example, often reflect the appropriate time of year. What would your pupils regard as typical of each season? What would they choose as a symbol of each season? Explain that sometimes artists have depicted each season as a person (usually a woman) and given her something appropriate to hold to show which season she represents. The Romans designed floor mosaics on this theme. At Osborne, your pupils will see four sculptures based on this idea. They will be looking at them before writing their own pieces, either prose or poetry, based on the four seasons.

Room				
SCALE	cosy	small	large	vast
ENCLOSURE	tight	enclosed	open	exposed
VARIETY	unvarying	simple	varied	complex
HARMONY	harmonious	balanced	discordant	chaotic
MOVEMENT	dead	calm	busy	frantic
COLOUR	one-colour	muted	colourful	garish
RARITY	ordinary	unusual	rare	unique
SECURITY	comfortable	safe	unsettling	threatening
STIMULUS	boring	bland	interesting	exciting
PLEASURE	nasty	unpleasant	pleasant	beautiful

The royal children acting in a tableau representing the seasons, 1854.

On site

Pupils could work individually, or in pairs or in small groups. Each individual or group will need four copies of the activity sheet – one for each season. Ask your pupils to identify the four statues on the parterre. How can you tell which is which? Look carefully at what each is holding. Are there any other clues?

Start with the season of your visit. Ask pupils to choose several things they can see from the position of the relevant sculpture: on the parterre or visible from the parterre. They should be recorded as nouns in the appropriate section of the activity sheet. Next they should add an adjective to each noun. Encourage pupils to choose things or descriptive words that fit the season.

Follow the *'I see'* section with what they can hear. *'I feel'* could be interpreted in terms of the temperature or the wind, or could refer to pupils' emotions: how the place makes them feel. Go through the same process for the other seasons, using imagination rather than observation or listening skills.

If you have time on site, continue by adding descriptive phrases. You could encourage pupils to use alliteration, choosing the initial sound of either the noun or the adjective and including at least one other word beginning with this sound. However, this would be quite a challenging task. Examples might be: fine rain falling on bright flowers; crunching footsteps of crowds of people. Alternatively, add these phrases back at school.

When you tour the house, point out to your pupils the sculptures of the royal children in the drawing room: they too are intended to represent the seasons. More difficult to see, but also relevant, is the photograph in Prince Albert's bathroom of a tableau of the royal children dressed as the seasons.

After the visit
Use the words and phrases, written during the visit, as the basis of imaginative writing on the seasons. The task could be individual or collaborative. If you wish you could provide a structure, specifying the number of lines or the number of stanzas for a poem, or asking pupils to write an acrostic – where the first letter of each line spells a word.

Osborne and the curriculum

English
The extraordinary visual impact of the house and its contents could be a stimulus to work on vocabulary. Look for suitable descriptive words to apply to the general impression given and to individual objects. Older pupils could try using the following sets of words, choosing the most appropriate from each group of four. You will need to reproduce the words – several copies for each pupil. As you tour the house, it should be possible for pupils to pause now and again to record the location and underline the most appropriate word from each group. (Possible pause-points might be the Council Chamber, the dining room and the Durbar Room.) This exercise illustrates the richness of the English language and demonstrates the possibility of recording individual impressions quite precisely.

Play charades, as the royal children did at Osborne. Divide the class into groups. Each group chooses a word of more than one syllable, which the others have to guess. Each syllable of the word is conveyed separately through a short dramatic scene, and then the whole word is used in the final scene. You could specify that the words have to relate to Osborne, or to the Victorians.

Mathematics
The educational approach *'Classical Collection'* includes mathematical activities based on the architecture and on the parterres on the seaward side of the house. The suggested work on trees involves calculations, and the information gathered could be presented in mathematical forms such as Venn diagrams.

Statistical information could be gathered for use back at school. This could be based on observation (the numbers of visitors using the carriage rides and the numbers walking at particular times; the number of visitors making use of seats at the front of the house), or it could be derived from question-naires, investigating for example, where visitors come from. (If you use questionnaires, make sure your pupils work in groups, have been thoroughly instructed and are well supervised. It would also be helpful to check first with English Heritage staff.)

Use the information to construct charts and graphs. Evaluate the work. Can you safely draw conclusions from it?

Science
Consider some of the issues involved in the conservation of historic objects. What problems are there in caring for the treasures in Osborne House? Did pupils notice anything during their tour which showed that an effort was being made to protect things? (You could think about light and fading, pests such as moth and woodworm, the upkeep of the building, security, the implications of a large number of visitors and the steps taken to deter them from touching fragile objects.)

The conservation theme could be extended to work on the estate, which is being restored to reflect Prince Albert's intention that it should be an example of good land management, with sustainable development and recycling of waste. One aspect of this work is the replanting of trees and the reintroduction of traditional management of the woodlands.

Visit the ice-house. Is the temperature inside it cooler than the air temperature outside? What is the insulating material? Back at school, test the effectiveness of earth as insulation: For example, dig a hole in a patch of earth, quickly pack some ice-cubes into a plastic container, put the container in the hole and fill in the earth over it. At the same time, pack the same number of ice-cubes into an identical container and leave in the open air. When the ice-cubes in the open air have melted, check the buried container and compare.

History
Osborne is a rich primary resource for the history study unit Victorian Britain. Actually seeing Osborne has a tremendous impact; the combination of sumptuous decoration with the homeliness of some of the personal possessions is memorable.

Most of the educational approa-ches suggested have a historical dimension. Other, problem-solving, approaches could be effective. For example you could set the following scenario for your pupils.

You have been asked to help with an exhibition on Queen Victoria: Which four objects would you choose to borrow and why? What would they tell people about the Queen? Write a label for each of the objects so that visitors to the exhibition will understand and appreciate them.

Geography

Use maps of the estate to practise map-reading and route-finding. Set supervised groups to follow particular routes, with questions about what can be seen at certain points. Alternatively, provide an outline plan, and ask pupils to record different kinds of land-use (grass, shrubberies, woodland, orchard, buildings) and features they will see (ice-house, pond, summer-house, seats).

Visual arts

Osborne contains many works of art – objects, pictures and sculptures – both inside and out. In some areas of the house it is possible to pause and study the pictures in small groups, for example in the dining room and the Indian corridor. Outside on the terraces spend time looking at the sculptures, some of them given by the Queen and Prince as presents to

which reflected his enthusiasm for inventiveness and technology. Osborne House was up to date, incorporating the relevant technology of the time. Both the house and its contents are a rich resource for work in design and technology. For practical reasons you may prefer to focus on the resources outside the house. The approach *'Classical Collection'* suggests an analysis of design features of the exterior architecture, followed by the designing of Italianate houses. Some pupils respond to more unusual assignments, so an alternative task could be to design an Italianate bus shelter or telephone box or umbrella stand. Also outside, the children's area of the estate could be studied (what elements of the design make it suitable for children?) and pupils could design their own children's gardens.

Music

Pupils could look for evidence during their tour of the house that Victoria and Albert were interested in music. They will find some corroboration in the documents.

The royal children sometimes put on a musical concert to celebrate their mother's birthday. Your class could learn some Victorian or traditional songs that could have been performed at Osborne. Another possibility for practical music would be an introduction to Indian instruments and composition in order to devise an Indian-style programme to accompany a banquet in the Indian Room.

Religious studies

Work on Osborne and the royal household may raise ethical issues in connection with the contrast between wealth and poverty, the rigidity of the social hierarchy of the time, and the implications of imperialism. The Queen's attitude to her servants and the Prince's idealistic ambitions for the estate and its workforce could be discussed. Though she could be difficult and capricious, the Queen was genuinely interested in the welfare of her staff; and Albert believed that individuals and society could be transformed if decent housing and education were universal.

The terrace at Osborne, sketched by Jamie Whaley, 12 years old, Osborne Middle School.

each other. Look for example at the Prince's dog, Eos, and the statues representing the four seasons.

The exterior of the house, the gardens, the terraces and the grounds could provide inspiration for your pupils' own works of art, in sketches or watercolours or as photographs. The Queen had instruction in watercolour painting from the artist Leitch, and practised her skills at Osborne.

Design and technology

Prince Albert was the inspiration behind the Great Exhibition,

Annotated drawing is an excellent method of recording design features and understanding them. Some of the objects in the house (perhaps those pictured on *Activity Sheet 3*) could be evaluated from the points of view of aesthetics and the suitability of the design for the purpose, or compared to their modern equivalents.

As it is possible to use the Durbar Room more flexibly, some of the decorative features could be recorded and used as an inspiration for designing items such as t-shirts, tea-towels, scarves and jewellery.

Cultural connections

The educational approach of The Indian connection focuses on the most obvious multi-cultural opportunity provided by Osborne. In addition, the estate illustrates the Victorian enthusiasm for plant-collecting of species from all over the world. The shrubberies at Osborne include large numbers of camellias, which were introduced from China, and rhododendrons, which were introduced from the Himalayas. Prince Albert planted trees from continental Europe, North and South America and Asia, as specimens in the garden and parkland. Good reference books on garden plants should provide information on the origin of some of the trees, shrubs, perennials and annuals in the gardens.

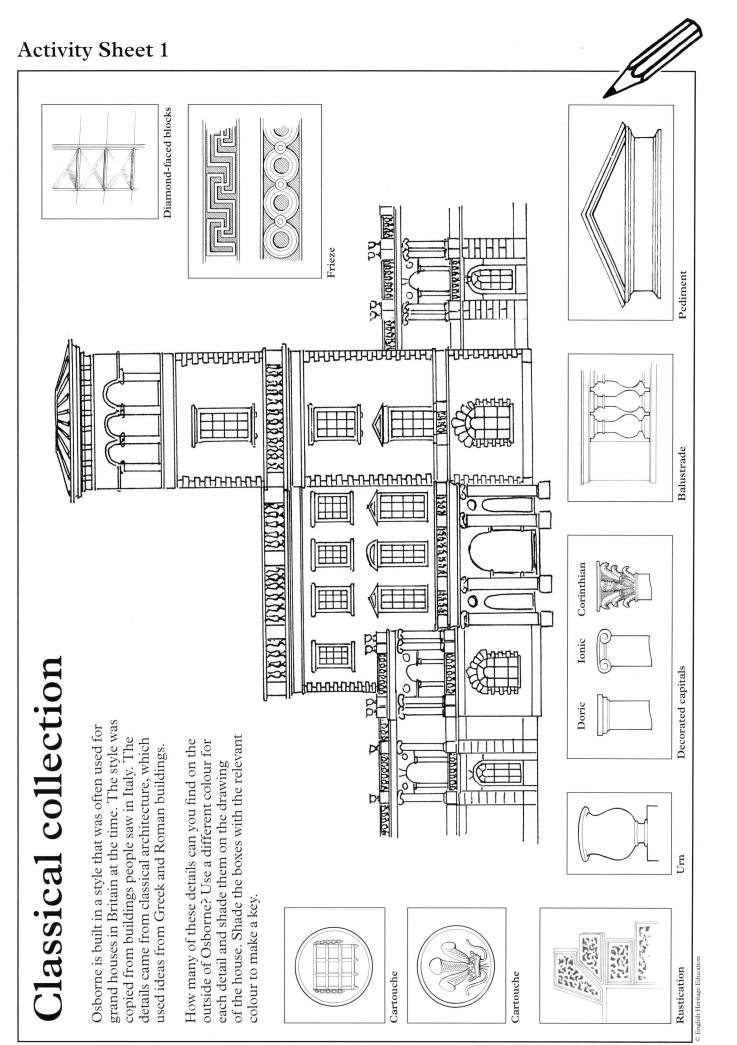

Classical collection

Osborne is built in a style that was often used for grand houses in Britain at the time. The style was copied from buildings people saw in Italy. The details came from classical architecture, which used ideas from Greek and Roman buildings.

How many of these details can you find on the outside of Osborne? Use a different colour for each detail and shade them on the drawing of the house. Shade the boxes with the relevant colour to make a key.

Diamond-faced blocks

Frieze

Pediment

Balustrade

Decorated capitals

Doric   Ionic   Corinthian

Urn

Cartouche

Cartouche

Rustication

Opinions of Osborne

Fill in what you think these people might say about Osborne. The unlabelled one at the end is for your own view.

Prince Albert

Lady in waiting

Household servant

An important visitor

Gardener

Out of the ordinary

Look out for these objects as you tour the house. As you find each of them, draw a line to one of the labels to show what it is made of.

The most surprising object I saw was

_____

The most interesting object I saw was

_____

antler

wood

silver

stone

ivory

glass

china

Tree study

Choose a tree to study carefully. Use this sheet to record as much information as possible about your tree.

Ring the word which describes your tree, or record the information on the chart below.

Position on site	sheltered open/exposed	sloping ground flat ground	wet ground dry ground
Surrounding environment	dense woodland parkland	thin woodland mown grass	scrub/bushes/brambles bare ground
Measurements	height	girth (1.5m from ground)	
Approximate age			
Shape	short spreading horizontal branches	tall narrow upright branches	 drooping branches
Management	natural clipped	pollarded pleached	coppiced

Leaf shape (sketch)	**Flower** (sketch)	**Fruit** (sketch)

Bark	rough furrowed	smooth colour	peeling
Commemorative plaque	Take a rubbing		
Identification			
Origin	British native	foreign (from which area?)	

The four seasons

In the parterre garden, there are four sculptures representing the four seasons. Each sculpture is holding something to tell you which season it is. Find the sculptures and work out which is which.

The sculptures stand in the garden all year round.

Imagine what they see and hear and feel at each season of the year.

Use your words and phrases for a piece of writing back at school.

SEASON:

noun   adjective

I see

I hear

I feel

SEASON:

noun   adjective

I see

I hear

I feel

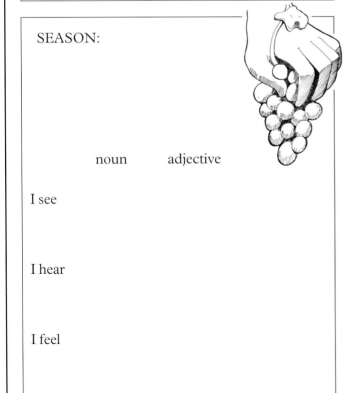

SEASON:

noun   adjective

I see

I hear

I feel

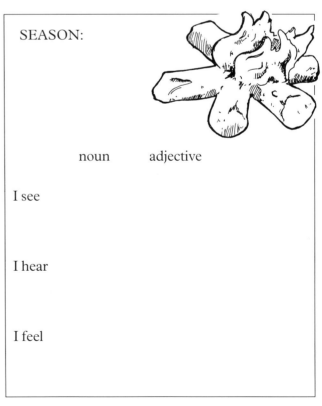

SEASON:

noun   adjective

I see

I hear

I feel

Bibliography and resources

Books marked* are suitable for pupils. Books marked** are from the Education on Site series for teachers.

Osborne

Hobhouse, H, *Thomas Cubitt: Master Builder*, Management Books, 1995, ISBN 1-85251-148-6.

Tolhurst, M, *Life on a Royal Estate*, a document pack for Osborne House, English Heritage, 1986, ISBN 1-85074-126-3.

Turner, M, *Osborne House*, English Heritage, 2000, ISBN 1-85074-249-9. Souvenir Guide.

Victoria and Albert

Longford, E, *Queen Victoria*, Abacus, 2000, ISBN 0-349-11255-X. A re-issue of the classic biography of Queen Victoria.

Longford, E, *Queen Victoria*, Sutton Publishing, 1999, ISBN 0-7509-2143-9. In the Sutton Pocket Biographies series, a biography covering the whole of Victoria's reign.

Sheffield, E, (ed), *Private Life of the Queen 1897*, Gresham Books, 1979, ISBN 0-905418-66-2. This book, originally published in 1987, was written anonymously by one of Queen Victoria's servants. It is now out of print, but you may be able to borrow it from your library.

Van der Kiste, J, *Queen Victoria's Children*, Alan Sutton, 1990, ISBN 0-86299-859-X.

Victorian life

Girouard, M, *The Victorian Country House*, Yale University Press, 1979, ISBN 0-300-034572-5.

*Hicks, P, *The Victorians*, Wayland, 1995, ISBN 0-75021-065-6.

Overy, C, *A teacher's guide to Charles Darwin: his life, journeys and discoveries*, English Heritage, 1997, ISBN 0-85074-688-0. This book gives an insight into the way of life of Darwin and his family, not regarded as typical Victorians.

*Wilson, L, *Daily Life in a Victorian House*, Hamlyn, 1995, ISBN 0-60058-684-7.

Victorians at work, National Monuments Record, 1998, ISBN 1-873592-43-4. This pack contains eight A3 photographs with teacher's notes.

Victorian Transport, English Heritage, 1999, ISBN 1-873592-46-9. Eight A3 photographs with teacher's notes.

Food and Cooking in Nineteenth-century Britain, English Heritage, 1985, ISBN 0-85074-539-0. This contains plenty of recipes for pupils to try.

Multi–cultural influences

Campbell, C, *The Maharajah's Box*, Harper Collins, 2000, ISBN 0-00257-008-4. The biography of Duleep Singh.

Guy, J & D, Swallow, *Arts of India 1550-1900*, Victoria and Albert Museum, 1990, ISBN 1-85177-022-4.

Educational approaches

**Primary History*, English Heritage, 1999, ISBN 0-85074-650-8. This book looks at how primary teachers can use the evidence of the past all around them to teach the history study units for Key Stages 1 and 2, including three sections on the Victorians.

**Allen, S, Hollinshead, L, & Wilkinson, S, *Using Houses and Homes*, English Heritage, 1998, ISBN 0-85074-398-3. Full of exciting ideas for looking at ordinary houses with your pupils.

**Barker, R & Marcus, S, *Historic Parks and Gardens*, English Heritage, 1997, ISBN 0-85074-510-2. This provides historical background to the development of gardens over time, as well as lots of suggestions for pupils' work, which may be adapted and used in the grounds at Osborne.

**Barnes, J, *Design and Technology and the Historic Environment*, English Heritage, 1999, ISBN 0-85074-399-1. Osborne provides many opportunities for your pupils to consider aspects of Victorian design and technology. This book provides a range or approaches to the subject.

**Collins, F & Hollinshead, L, *English and the Historic Environment*, English Heritage, 2000, ISBN 0-85074-330-4. Offers ideas for using a visit to any historic site to develop your pupils skills in writing, reading, speaking and listening.

**Durbin, G, *Using Historic Houses*, English Heritage, 1993, ISBN 0-85074-390-8. This looks at the chronology of historic houses, including some Victorian examples, and provides ideas for approaches to work.

**Lockey, M, & Walmsley, D, *Art and the Historic Environment*, English Heritage, 1999, ISBN 0-85074-651-6. This full colour book aims to inspire teachers with examples of the creative art work their pupils can produce.

**Morris, S, *Using Portraits*, English Heritage, 1989, ISBN 0-85074-231-6. There are many portraits of Queen Victoria and her family, both at Osborne and in museums and galleries across the country. This book gives suggestions for using these portraits as a teaching resource.

Acknowledgements

This revised version of the handbook for teachers for Osborne owes a great deal to the research carried out for the original handbook, written by Marilyn Tolhurst.

Back cover: decorative detail in the Durbar Room.

English Heritage is the national leader in heritage education. We aim to help teachers at all levels to use the resource of the historic environment. Each year, we welcome over half a million pupils, students and teachers to over 400 historic sites in our care. For free copies of our **Free Educational Visits** booklet, our **Resources** catalogue, and **Heritage Learning,** our termly magazine, contact:

**English Heritage Education
Freepost 22 (WD 214)
London W1E 7EZ
Tel: 020-7973 3442
Fax: 020-7973 3443
www.HeritageEducation.net**